SHANIA
FEEL LIKE A WOMAN

ANDREW VAUGHAN

First published in Great Britain in 2000 by
Andre Deutsch Ltd
76 Dean Street
London W1V 5HA

www.vci.co.uk

1 3 5 7 9 10 8 6 4 2

A catalogue record for this title is available from the British Library

ISBN 0 233 999902 7

Printed in the UK by Butler & Tanner, Frome and London

CONTENTS

'It was never my dream to be a star, that was my parents' dream. I guess they prayed real hard.'

Shania Twain, 1998

FOREWORD

I first interviewed Shania Twain in 1993. At the time she was just another new singing star fresh to Nashville. I recall, though, being struck that she was one of the few celebrities I had met who looked better in person than on camera. She had a radiant, natural beauty which seemed to captivate all those around her. Talking to her then, in Nashville, after the release of her first album, it was clear this was one tough woman. She was sweet and gracious but knew exactly what she wanted. She complained, at the time, of not feeling accepted by Nashville, of not being understood.

She subsequently quickly became a star on Country Music Television in Europe, where I was PR Director for a couple of years. She was easily the most popular act on the station and we unashamedly used her profile in all our marketing efforts across Europe.

I met Shania on several occasions after that first time and was struck by her resolute determination as well as a hint of detachment and maybe sadness behind those haunting eyes. It was as though there were two people present within Shania Twain, and maybe there were; Eileen Edwards, as she was born, seems to have been a quite different person to the Shania Twain she became. The last time I saw her, I wondered whether Eileen, the sensitive, self-conscious kid of the 1970s, had perhaps given too much of herself to Shania in the 1990s. Was the sacrifice worth it? She was the biggest country star in the world, but she looked a shade lost and lonely at the CMA Awards in 1999 when her husband, Robert John 'Mutt' Lange, didn't show for the ceremony. In this book I have traced her story, drawn on past interviews, talked with those who were involved and who know her, and attempted to throw some light on the personal psyche of a poor kid from Canada who forced her way to becoming the most successful female country music artist of all time.

Shania Twain, the Canadian singing star with the film-star looks, has single-handedly turned country music on its head in the last five years. Her records have dominated both the country and the pop charts in the US and in the past year she has begun to sell millions of albums around the world, especially in the UK, where the country singer was recently at number one in both the singles and album charts and sold a record-breaking 60,000 long form videos.

With her trademark bared midriff (previously an absolute no-no in country music) and blatant flaunting of her sexuality on music videos, she has moved from being the top-selling female in country music to a bona fide pop superstar in an incredibly short space of time. In the US she has surprised the Nashville community by winning legitimacy from the rock establishment when she appeared on the cover of *Rolling Stone* magazine (a feat matched previously only by Tanya Tucker and Garth Brooks), and not since the golden days of Dolly Parton has a female country singer so captured the hearts of the world.

Incredibly, her life has been an almost classic rags-to-riches story which reads like a country and western song. Raised in abject poverty in rural Canada, life was tough, but worse was to come when her parents were both killed in a car accident. Shania, or Eileen, as she was called then, took responsibility for her younger siblings. She was just twenty-two years old.

Her mother's dreams of Eileen having a singing career, to which both parents had held since Eileen had been a tiny kid, were put on hold. Eventually, when her younger brothers were old enough to look after themselves, Eileen moved to Nashville. She won herself a record deal and changed her name to Shania, but not much happened immediately. She was just another pretty girl singer doing what her Nashville bosses told her to do.

And then her world turned on its axis. A mystery phone call one night would prove to be the catalyst for an explosive few years ahead. The caller was record producer and songwriter 'Mutt' Lange, the man responsible for producing many top rock acts of the 1980s, among them Def

Leppard, Foreigner, AC/DC and, more recently, Bryan Adams. He wanted to talk to Shania. Several weeks of late-night phone calls, talking mostly about music, ended with Mutt producing Shania's next album and the couple getting married. It was a fairy tale, especially when that album, *The Woman In Me*, ripped the country – and then pop music – charts apart. From nowhere she was outselling Madonna, Michael Jackson and Hootie & the Blowfish. From that moment on, Shania continued to outgrow Nashville without, for most of the time, winning their approval. That country music industry rejection of her career was arguably the most persistent disappointment of the first five years. But even the conservative forces of Nashville were eventually won over by the Canadian's power of performance, strength of will and enormous sales: in late 1999 Shania won both their acceptance and the prestigious CMA Female Vocalist of the Year Award.

When the young Eileen Twain adopted an Indian name, Shania, meaning 'I'm on my way' in 1991, fate and fortune seemingly chose to turn her life around. This is the story of how it all happened.

Andrew Vaughan
Nashville, April 2000

N.B. For clarity's sake, I have referred to Eileen when necessary and Shania likewise in the text, sometimes within the space of a sentence. This is deliberate and meant to convey the differences between both sides of the same person.

CHAPTER ONE

GOD BLESS THE CHILD

Unlike many country music legends, Shania Twain wasn't born in a mountain home in the Appalachian or Smoky Mountains, nor was she raised on a cattle ranch in Texas. No, the most famous and most commercially successful artist in country music was born in Canada. In Windsor, Ontario, to be precise, on 28 August 1965. Nor was she called Shania – her given name was Eilleen Regina Edwards (presumably the Royal middle moniker was in recognition of her birthplace). She would change Edwards to Twain when her mother remarried. Eilleen remained in Canada until she signed her first record deal in Nashville in 1991.

Her biological father, Clarence Edwards, and her mother Sharon had three children, all girls: Eilleen was the second born, a couple of years after Jill and three years before Carrie-Ann. Little is known about Clarence – except that he was of French-Irish extraction and worked as a railway engineer – or why the marriage failed. He has remained distant from Eilleen and has not (so far) spoken to the press. In interviews Shania has suggested that Clarence, whom she can hardly have known since he left her life when she was little more than three years old, was never a 'real' dad to her in the way that her adopted father, Gerald Twain was. As an adult she chose not to bear any of the names given to her by her biological father; to all intents and purposes she was – or is – a different person altogether to Eilleen Edwards.

As is nearly always the case when contemplating the life and career of a star of any kind, there are times when the true identity of the person behind the public façade is hard to spot. This is sometimes the case with Shania Twain. There are very obvious and contrasting differences between who Eilleen Edwards, and who Shania Twain is – Shania can gyrate suggestively on a video screen, for instance, while Eilleen admits, 'I'm not that physical. I'm not a sexual person. My mind isn't there. I mean, I'm very satisfied and I'm not hard to satisfy. Always had total control of my sexual habits.' There are also obviously times when they are in complete harmony. The comment about having 'total control' for instance, is something that Eilleen displayed a desire for

David Anderson/Corbis

from a young age. Before Shania had been invented, Eilleen had several professional identities in her eventful life. There is no doubting Eilleen/Shania's overriding ambition to succeed on her own terms and not at any cost, and it is clear that this ambition was fostered in her by her mother, who was tragically killed when Eilleen was about to begin a glorious singing career.

It is possible that the key to Eilleen/Shania's success lies in the establishing of a single-minded

purpose by both her mother and events over which Eilleen had no control: the loss of family is a huge emotional blow to anyone, and Eilleen/Shania has suffered doubly in her life. One can only guess at the damage that the loss of a parent has on a small child and although Eilleen undoubtedly came to regard Jerry as her true father, one can speculate about the existence in her of a lingering sense of loss over the departure of Clarence from her life.

Not long after the birth of Carrie-Ann, Sharon and Clarence split up. Four years later, Sharon married Ojibwa forest worker Jerry Twain, who then adopted the children. They lived in Timmins, Ontario. A small town in the middle of nowhere, surrounded by forest and rivers, it sits amid beautiful countryside that is as glorious in the warm summers as it is harshness itself in the 40-degrees-below freezing winters.

Founded in 1912 as an encampment to serve the goldrush which had begun five years earlier, Timmins has always been a mining community first (mining still accounts for the majority of employment) and a logging town second. The gold had been found along the shore of the Porcupine Lake and Frederick House River (named after first prospector Frederick Schumacher) and by 1911 had proved enough of a draw to eager prospectors that the railway arrived. By then there were plenty of successful mines and there must have been the usual collection of greed-crazed wildmen, decent, hardworking people, opportunistic conmen, illegal and legal booze traders, trappers and dealers who gathered around each and every boomtown in the North-West at that time. According to the Timmins City information board, within two days of the railway arriving in the town (named after Noah Timmins, an early and successful settler), a fire raged through the clapboard and canvas camp, totally destroying it. Because the gold was still there, though, the camp was swiftly rebuilt and continued to grow. The people of Timmins are a hardy bunch, it seems.

The Depression of the 1930s never got that far north and by the time the gold ran out in the mid-twentieth century, other base metals had been discovered, the lumber industry was flourishing and the population had grown to around 50,000. Today Timmins is enjoying a new influx of trade and foreign money; tourism has hit big, solely thanks to its most famous daughter, Shania Twain.

However, back in the early 1970s, Sharon and Jerry struggled for money. 'We were real poor,' Shania says; 'it was common for us to go for days with just bread and milk. Times were very harsh.' Jerry has been described as working both in the mines and the forests, never being employed in one place for too long. The reasons for this are probably due to his ethnic origin and unfortunately only being able to get seasonal employment. Times were not as enlightened then as they are now and Eilleen found herself and by this time four siblings (Sharon and Jerry had two sons, Mark and Darryl) being moved around the Timmins–Sudbury area following the work. According to Shania, Jerry refused to go on the dole, and sought work wherever he could.

Later, after she'd started at high school, Eilleen, from the age of thirteen, would work in the summer for Jerry who had, with his brothers and parents, formed a logging company. While promoting her first Mercury Nashville CD release, Shania would say that she spent summer holidays working as a foreman in the forests, 'leading' a team of thirteen men. This seems unlikely, given her tender age. It is more likely that Jerry had such a logging crew and that Eilleen would go out into the forest with him and the team and get to wield an axe and a chainsaw. Whatever the case, clearly by her teen years times can't have been as bad in the Twain household as they had been in the early 1970s.

Prior to those teenage summer logging days, it was cold in the Ontario winters and, unable to pay their heating bills, it was not uncommon for the Twain family to sit huddled around the wood-burning stove of an evening, trying desperately to keep warm. Layers of clothes and heavy coats were used as makeshift blankets when it came time to sleep. 'I don't really remember if I was aware of how harsh things were at the time,' she told me in 1995, 'but looking back it was hard, especially for the kids. My parents did the best they could, we all knew that, and we made the best of everything but I can clearly remember having no food in the house. It's not a feeling I ever want to experience again. But I do remember the feeling of community; family members would send us food packages, beaver and moose meat usually, and that kept us going through the worst times.'

With no luxuries to speak of, Eilleen's childhood centred on nature and her imagination. She became a creative child, inventing games and creating characters in her head. And with her adoptive father teaching her all he knew about the forest and wildlife, hunting and trapping for food, the forest became her playground. Impressed by her love of singing, her parents gave Eilleen a beaten-up old guitar that became the youngster's constant companion. She'd take it everywhere, down to the river to write songs, build a campfire and drift away into the darkness making up her own tunes and words. 'I loved music, I always have. I guess it just took me to another place, to a fantasyland where people were rich and happy and warm and had lots of food. It was an escape in my mind in some ways but it was always a very vital part of who I was. I literally sang all the time as I recall.'

Sharon encouraged her second daughter and began to hope that the she might just make it as a singer. Amazed at her ability to mimic the country stars she heard on the radio and eight-track cartridges that would be played on the seemingly interminable car journeys across country to another mine or forest, Sharon began to encourage Eilleen to learn the songs properly. With money so tight it's not uncommon for even the youngest family member to be expected to earn whatever they could to help put food on the table. In low-income families children would work chores for neighbours, run errands for local shops, work in fast-food joints when old enough and occasionally (if the child showed enough talent) they would even be able to perform for money.

'As far as my career as a child [went],' Shania told *Canada's Hot New Country* magazine for their Winter 1996 edition, 'the only music we had in the house for me to learn from were eight-track country tapes.' So Eilleen learned country tunes: Dolly Parton, Patsy Cline, Johnny Cash, the kind of stuff that would enable her to perform in front of a variety of audiences, from old people's homes to after-hours bar crowds. At the age of eight Eilleen would make regular appearances after 1 a.m. in the bar of a hotel on a local Indian reservation, the Hotel Matagami, for twenty dollars a gig. 'I never liked any of that,' she told *Canada's Hot New Country*; 'I liked singing but I didn't understand why I had to do it in the middle of the night.' Sharon did, though. It wasn't much money but for a poverty-stricken family every little helped. Because of the licensing laws, the young Eilleen had to sing after one in the morning when they'd finished serving alcohol. 'They'd wake me in the middle of the night, I'd get dressed up in a home-made deerskin cowgirl outfit and go sing. My mother was determined to make a singer out of me,' Shania recalled.

This makes Sharon sound like a dreadful 'stage Mom' – determined to make a star out of her little girl at any cost. And maybe she was, but that determination was born out of love, need and a burning desire to see her child have a better life than she had known, which Eilleen understands and appreciates. 'I would never be where I am now without her dedication and her sacrifices in those early days.'

When it wasn't the Hotel Matagami, Eilleen's mother made the rounds of social clubs, TV stations, newspapers and radio stations promoting her little girl as a star. Shania told Kimmy Wix of *Music City News* magazine in 1995, 'We went to every TV station, every radio station, every community centre, every senior citizen centre. They had me doing everything.'

All of which was great training as Eilleen would realize later in life. By her early teen years the 'everything' had grown to include other music styles. She had begun writing songs almost as soon as she could sing, making up her own tunes to nursery rhymes, picking out melody lines on her old guitar and listening to the only radio station in Timmins, which played all kinds of music: country, western, pop, rock, jazz and even classical.

If the musical education Eilleen received in any way interfered with her scholastic learning, it is not obvious. One can only suppose that things must have been tough at junior school, though. The moving around can't have been conducive to establishing good friendships or teacher–pupil relationships, plus Shania has commented about her early school life, that she would carry mustard or mayonnaise sandwiches (no other filling) to lunch and hide their content in case anyone thought that her parents could not manage with five children and so split the family up. Given that the majority of the town's populace in which she grew up were white, blue-collar and carried all the usual prejudices that went with that, there could well have been some degree of racist abuse put upon her and more likely her younger brothers. Shania has not commented much on any such treatment publicly except to have recorded, in the late 1980s, a song entitled 'Half-Breed' in which she sings about how she'd been hearing the name half-breed all her life and hating it (the song had been a hit single for Cher in 1973). She also told Barbara Hager for her book *Honour Song: A Tribute* (Raincoast Books, 1996; reprinted in *On Her Way: The Life and Music of Shania Twain*, Berkeley Boulevard, 1998), 'I encountered racism growing up. Sometimes we were the only native family in the neighbourhood. I stuck up for myself and my brothers. There was one time when I was in my teens and the parents of a boy I was dating made him stop seeing me because I was native.'

By the time Eilleen reached high school she was remarkably level-headed and into any and all kinds of music, and that meant that she quickly became popular with both boys and girls.

19

CHAPTER TWO

IF YOU WANT TO TOUCH HER, ASK!

Timmins High and Vocational School is a solid, respectable and unremarkable school, just like thousands of others in Canada. It offers its students a solid start in all the subjects that one would expect, including music. One of her former classmates, now a Timmins lawyer, recalled his days in music class with Eilleen for the *Timmins Daily Press*. Calvin Ferrier, a duty counsel with Legal Aid Ontario, took Grade Eleven instrumental music class, instructed by Joe Belinkis. He, another student and Twain each played trumpet. Teacher Belinkis tried to get the three to alternate playing first (the hardest part) trumpet. 'Me and Ron Randall were lazy,' Ferrier told his local paper in 1999. 'We preferred the easier third trumpet part so we always got Eilleen to play the more difficult first part.' Eilleen was obviously unfazed by it all. 'Music stardom was her destiny,' says the lawyer plainly. Another ex-pupil at Timmins High proudly displayed his graduation yearbook for the paper. He proved to be particularly pleased with an inscription from Eilleen which reads, 'I don't have a funny rhyme to write so I'll be serious. You're the most serious friend I've got. Remember me when I'm famous and I'll remember you,' (signed Eilleen Twain). Next to Twain's inscription, the paper said, another student has scribbled a rather typical, cynical two-letter response: 'Ha.'

Offering proof, if it be needed, that by the time she was eighteen, Eilleen knew wholeheartedly what she wanted from life, Olaf Karls, the yearbook's owner, told the *Daily Press* that, 'She always knew she was going to be successful. Some people call that bravado, I call it confidence.'

It is a view backed up in the *Daily Press* by her Grade Ten maths teacher, Gord Spylo, who told them that he 'saw the development of the skills and character traits which would propel Twain to stardom.' He went on to say, 'She was a pleasant, hard-working, conscientious student who got her school-work done, even when doing so conflicted with concert gigs,' adding, 'I saw this in the early stages in my high school math class. She was pleasant, wonderful, a really nice student.' He then uttered the one word used by adults meaning to praise students, but which is guaranteed to

make the student squirm with embarrassment: 'Keen', he said. And clearly, she was. It is unusual in examining the life and career of a truly famous person, not to find somebody who has an axe to grind, a dig to get in, someone who was jilted, rejected, fooled, made to feel less significant than the now famous person, who wants to get their revenge in. But with Shania Twain, everyone seems to have only good memories of what must have been difficult years.

Olaf Karls's summation of Eilleen Twain the high school student is the commonly held view: 'Shania is tremendously talented and just plain nice. It's great to see her make it.'

Eilleen's teenage years, while being financially at least a little easier than her childhood, were still complicated. She showed concentration and diligence in every part of her life and took on a number of menial jobs at fast-food outlets and so on, but treated it all as if it was a training ground. She learned the merits of focus and concentration, while the physical work she would witness and participate in in the timber industry in the summers taught her the benefits of a healthy mind and a healthy body.

Something of an awkward teenager, Shania later recalled that she tried to deny her sexuality during her puberty and hid her body beneath 'layers of shirts . . . three at a time, and baggy trousers'. As she told *Rolling Stone* magazine in September 1998, tellingly adopting the non-personal third-person vernacular, 'The guy sees a girl who's developed up there, maybe they touch you up there and you really feel very invaded. And so, you know what? The easiest thing is to just cover them up, trying to get rid of the bounce factor.' Which seems incredibly prissy for someone who would so successfully exploit her sexuality in selling her records. But of course the Shania Twain on the video screen in the late 1990s is not directly related to the Eilleen Twain who would hang out with the guys in Timmins at the end of the 1970s and the beginning of the 1980s, going to Pink Floyd gigs and pretending to be Pat Benatar on stage in front of her high school pals. The halting fumbles of teenage boys in Eilleen Twain's life were, much like other aspects of her existence, something to be endured until she was fully in control and could do what she wanted. As her mother had taught her, Eilleen needed the power to go her own way and that power was only likely to come from this unique talent she had to sing and make music.

Sensibly, Shania steered clear of the drink and drugs which were very common at that time (and are even more so now) in any small town, anywhere in the western world – even Ontario. She simply didn't want or need to partake of any of the artificial highs that seemed so readily available at the time. The glamorous counter-culture of the 1960s and the legacy of Woodstock held great sway in North America long after the dream had died a bloody death at Altamont Speedway, killed by knife-wielding Hell's Angels at a free Rolling Stones concert. It was especially true among teenagers with little to keep them occupied except dreams of hot summer days, free love and mind-expanding drugs.

Shania did not need her mind psychotropically expanded, though, as she told *Rolling Stone*: 'The music was so good: Supertramp, Rush and Pink Floyd. I'm like, "You guys want to put a few things on your tongue, do acid, you just go ahead." Meanwhile I probably look high. I used to really rock out. I'd get people coming up to me, saying "Do you do drugs, or what?" I never did, I just looked like I did.' So much about Shania was different, even if she did try to hide that difference from her friends. Her musical taste, which sounds a little 'dodgy' in the previous statement ('good'? Supertramp?!?), was actually a lot more eclectic and interesting than that of many of her friends.

As a small child she talked about her mother wearing a beehive, which goes some way to demonstrate how behind everything Canada was – by the end of the 1960s the beehive had been dormant as a style statement for as long as the quiff – and her singing along with Stevie Wonder, Gladys Knight and the Carpenters. 'I never wanted to be a star, I wanted to be Stevie Wonder's backup singer,' she told one interviewer. 'I used to pray, "Please God, I want Stevie Wonder to hear me sing."' And yet, as was the case for any teenager who wanted to fit in socially at that time, Eilleen was willing and able to get down with some pretty plodding prog rock and even see the attraction of a live band building a huge blank wall in front of them as they played live gigs (Pink Floyd – *The Wall*), or listen to ear-splitting overlong guitar solos played by men with hair that looked like a dead poodle.

In fact, as events seem to bear out, Eilleen was more than just a passing fan of ear-splitting rock. The first album's-worth of material she would record (see Chapter Three) is full of such six-stringed pomp. Her co-writer and producer at that time (1989), Paul Sabu, was during the mid- to late 1980s a minor AOR god, complete with leather jacket with sleeves rolled up to the elbow. So it wasn't surprising when, in the mid-1990s, Shania said that she loved everything that her future producer and husband Robert John 'Mutt' Lange had produced, since he had almost single-handedly invented the stadium pomp-rock genre of the 1980s with Def Leppard and Foreigner.

Back in the early 1980s, though, Eilleen's sense of responsibility, instilled in her at that young age when she pretended to have food in her lunchbox at school lest the authorities spot the crisis and split up her family, was making her a very dedicated young woman. Still faced with financial hardship, her family needed her to earn money. When she wasn't flipping burgers in McDonald's at night she sang in Top Forty covers bands in the local area, adapting her voice to a variety of styles and winning praise and a small following in the region. At sixteen she joined a local band called Longshot, and they played cover versions of the hits of the day – Canadian AOR hits, that is – the usual guitar-led rock of the time, besides Pat Benatar, maybe minor guitar god Robin Trower, and certainly the songs of the bands that her husband-to-be had produced. They'd usually play for cash at high schools, parties, or anywhere they could get a booking. Before long they were playing original numbers which Eilleen helped to write. 'I had the big hair and the outfits, it was very glam, and we had a blast,' Shania recalled later. 'I really did love singing pop music as much as country. It was different and taught me things about style and presentation that I know have stayed with me over the years.'

Still, her mother was pushing and encouraging Eilleen's musical ambitions. It seemed to be working. Eilleen had been focused on country music for a while when, around 1982, she had been taken to Nashville by a local Ontario band manager and had recorded a few country songs as demos. At that time Nashville wasn't particularly 'into' rock-oriented music. The 'outlaw' acts that Shania had grown up listening to such as Johnny Paycheck (she had loved his 'Take This Job And Shove It'), Waylon Jennings, Merle Haggerd and even Johnny Cash were in decline. Although never as musically rock-oriented as later country superstars like Garth Brooks, the 'outlaw breed', as they came to be known, (which also included Willie Nelson and Kris Kristofferson) had an attitude that was 'rock-style' in that it was anti-establishment, rebellious and sometimes irreverent. Which meant, of course, that it was extremely appealing to young, strong-willed country fans like Eilleen. From the late 1960s until the end of the 1970s, country music had enjoyed a thriving alternative market led by the outlaws. However, by the beginning of the 1980s, when a recession hit the whole of the music industry, Nashville had decided that it could only support the mainstream mainstay of its industry. Instead of men in black who snarled and laughed, Nashville preferred the bland orchestrations of the Mandrell Sisters with their matching cowgirl outfits, high hair, huge eyelashes and firm belief in a traditional way of doing things. It was all very predictable in a country which had recently chosen a former governor of California with a fervent belief in the death penalty for their president – albeit one who had previously enkoyed an acting career as sidekick to a chimpanzee. In the more liberal Canada, however, country music fans still liked their rough-edged, rockin' country music. Which is possibly why, not for the last time, the country music capital showed no interest in Shania's work. Clearly there was too much attitude in her music, or something. Obviously disappointed, on her return to Timmins, Eilleen went back to gigging with Longshot, singing rock songs.

Perhaps Sharon sensed that she was losing the country versus rock battle with her daughter but whatever the reason, after Eilleen graduated, Sharon felt that she had to do something to turn Eilleen back toward Nashville. So she called someone whom she hardly knew, but whom she felt might just turn her daughter back towards country music.

Around the time of her move to Timmins High, Eilleen and Sharon had met Mary Bailey, a professional country singer who, despite being Canadian (this was at a time when you had to be born south of the Mason–Dixon line in order to get any success as a country singer) had scored some hits in her homeland. As Mary would later recall, she'd been impressed by the then thirteen-

year-old Eilleen's performance on the bill they shared in Sudbury in 1978. Mary was impressed enough to remember Eilleen well when called upon by Sharon in 1984 to help with guiding the fledgling singer's career. For her part, Eilleen must have been impressed by the experienced and successful older woman's encouragement. The call to Bailey by Sharon was shrewd – surely Bailey would help to get Eilleen interested in country music again?

For a while that was the case. Mary called people she knew in Nashville, got Eilleen gigs singing country, and they even made another trip to Nashville. And once again Nashville rejected the woman who was to become the single most successful singer in the history of country music. After a couple of years, Mary and Eilleen called it a day and parted amicably. Eilleen returned to a career singing rock songs around Timmins and Sudbury with the taste of disappointment once more souring her mouth. She had seen and experienced a life outside the small confines of the admittedly beautiful north Ontario, and she wanted more. By the beginning of 1987, aged twenty-one, Eilleen Twain had decided to make the move away from the safety net of her family and all the friends she'd made. She travelled to Toronto to begin a new and, she hoped, more successful life as a singer.

However, fate was about to intervene in the cruellest way. Before she could begin any kind of musical career, having settled into a secretarial job to pay the rent, Eilleen received a phone call from her younger sister that would change her life for ever. It would bring about the greatest test of Eilleen's character. That she was able to cope so admirably with that test, an event that would have broken most families into little pieces, is proof of her determination to succeed – on her terms, and not at any cost.

CHAPTER THREE

I'M HOLDIN' ON TO LOVE

No matter what had gone before in her short life, no matter how unusual her upbringing, how irregular her home life, nothing can have prepared Eilleen for the short, distraught phone call she received from her younger sister on the night of 1 November 1987. Not even coming to terms with the loss of her biological father could have helped her cope with the terrible news she was about to receive. With no other way to say it, Carrie-Ann came straight out and told her that Sharon and Jerry had been in an accident in their Chevy Suburban and were both dead. Her brother Darryl, also in the car, had survived the impact of a logging lorry which had jack-knifed across the highway into their path.

'There are moments in life,' she told me in 1995, 'when you don't think, you just act. I don't think I knew what I was thinking or feeling but I headed back home from Toronto to take care of my family. It was all I could think about. They needed me and I was going to be there for them. There was so much to organize and take care of that I don't think the reality of losing both parents just like that really hit home for quite a time. I was the parent from that point on. I was only twenty-one, but I did what I could.'

This cruel event would overshadow every achievement of her soon-to-be-immense career. Whenever a new territory opened up for Shania Twain in the 1990s she would have to answer the same questions about that cold night. Or at least suffer newspapers digging up and reprinting comments she'd previously made about the event. As late as June 1999 she apparently told England's biggest-selling tabloid newspaper that 'I dream about them sometimes and maybe they are watching over me and seeing my success. I just hope that they are happy wherever they are but I miss them. One of my biggest regrets is that they never saw my success – I would have liked them to have shared it and experienced it.'

Understandably, while there were so many administrative things to take care of, Eilleen put her feelings and her ambitions to one side while she dealt with the reality of having to take care of her

All Action/Suzan Moore

32

family. Older sister Jill was married with small children at this point, so Eilleen, as the next oldest, took charge.

Having been made executor of the estate, Eilleen settled business affairs, arranged the funeral and took charge of Mark, fourteen, and Darryl, thirteen. Then she had to think about how to support her family. It wasn't going to be easy. Her job as a secretary was in Toronto where rents were high and such wages low. She could probably make more money singing, but where? Eilleen confronted the problem in the only way she knew. In a move that would have echoes later in her career, she called her former manager Mary Bailey. Not that asking for help was easy, as she'd unwittingly reveal in a later interview when she said, 'I'm very independent. I've always been very bold, straightforward and black 'n' white about things in everyday life.' Yet, practically, she explained, 'I like to simplify things, get to the facts. That's always been the way I've been and nothing has ever been able to distract me.' In the most telling statement about her character, Shania admitted that 'It's almost an insensitive quality,' qualifying it with: 'When you're raised poor, and you've got lots of responsibilities as a child, you just end up that way, and it actually can be a bitter thing, but when my parents died, it just made me realize how valuable life is, how really fragile life is.'

Mary was happy to hear from her former charge and was to prove invaluable, allowing Eilleen to cope with her new-found responsibility and continue her singing career by suggesting that she looked for work in a nightclub. There was no reason she had to give up music as long as she had regular and local work available to her. Mary found her a singing engagement at a holiday resort 150 miles (240km) north of Timmins, in Deerhurst. It was perfect, offering regular work, decent pay, and she was able to move her siblings with her to the resort town. Moreover, the experience allowed her to delve into yet another musical scenario.

Her new audience were more upscale than anything she'd experienced previously and were apparently immediately appreciative of her sweet vocals and warm stage persona. Eilleen got to work in a whole new musical genre, too – 'Off-Broadway' as she would call it later. It was a revue-style show which was, she said, 'a great experience. I had so much to learn. I didn't know how to work an audience, I wasn't used to wearing that stuff – you know, fishnets and high heels, it was all a strange new world to me. And we had stage managers and choreographers. I was used to playing seedy little country bars. It was a lot to take in, but luckily the people there liked me and I learned very quickly. I've always been a quick learner.'

It was here that Eilleen really discovered the Shania in her, the former shy teenager learning the power of her sexuality on stage. Eilleen became Shania not just physically but also emotionally and professionally. It was here that she met the Canadian Indian woman whose name was Shania, which Eilleen liked so much, especially on learning that it meant 'on my way'. After a while in the chorus it seems that Eilleen was given a featured spot in the 'Broadway' show as well as several numbers in the country and pop shows that were rotated with the revue. So she still got to sing other, sometimes rock-based and country, music during slots at the resort, in front of different audiences. All of which was a musical and performance education that not even Dolly Parton had a chance to experience.

Eilleen learned how to truly become someone else on stage, someone that strangers liked, regardless of whether they were fans of one style of music or another. Her looks – which she'd played down in the small jukejoints and bars at which she'd pretended to be Pat Benatar in front of half-drunk rockers – became a distinct advantage. As she'd tell *Playgirl* magazine (how Nashville's strait-laced guardians of moral decency must have been shocked by that) in October 1998, referring back to her teen years, 'I wanted to be strong and independent and at school, if

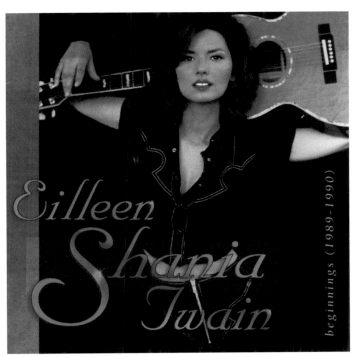

Courtesy Jomato Records

beginnings (1989-1990)

The sleeve of the US release
of Shania's first recordings,
made when she was still
known as Eilleen.

34

you had breasts and bounced and were feminine, people didn't see anything else. I'd wear loose
clothing and squash my breasts – what a waste that was. I should've been proud that I was female
and tried to change *their* perception.' On that stage in Deerhurst, Eilleen Twain was very female
and very proud. Later in her career she would reiterate that pride in her femininity by showing her
female form, regardless of the consequences. 'If people choose to see me only as a sex symbol, it's
their problem,' she told *Playgirl*; 'I'm not going to be less of a woman just so people don't
overlook my brains. That's a great injustice to women.'

Over those three years, during the day Eilleen was to all intents and purposes a working Mom.
Often though, just as things were looking good, bills would come in, her brothers would need new
clothes or books, and money was an issue all over again. Still, Eilleen knew a trick or two about
surviving on next to nothing and if she had to wash clothes in the stream again, as her mother had
fifteen years before, then so be it. She was a proper Mom, taking the boys to school in the
mornings, picking them up in the afternoons and looking after the household. She also had to deal
with the emotions of two teenagers who had recently lost their parents. Which mostly meant that
she would have to disregard her own, of course. As she later revealed, 'I was so miserable but

there was nothing I could do about it, so I didn't allow myself to grieve for a year,' which is a painfully long time to hold in such strong emotions. When asked by a British newspaper in 1999 what her greatest fear was, Eilleen replied, 'Someone in my life dying. I know what it's like and it's a very scary thing.' Talking about that time to *Rolling Stone* magazine she said, 'I became very hard for quite a long time. I was so numb. Nothing penetrated. It was a very difficult time. But boy oh boy, did I ever get strong!'

A physical sign of the hardness she had just developed was offered in late 1999 when remixed tapes of recordings that Eilleen made some time in 1989 and 1990 surfaced. Released in America on the Jomato label as *Eilleen Shania Twain Beginnings 1989–1990*, and in the UK as *Wild & Wicked*, the sleeve notes (on the UK edition) drew comparisons between Shania and The Beatles: 'It is not unknown for an artist who later achieved world fame to be unappreciated at the beginning of their career.' It continued, 'One good example is The Beatles, whose early record productions were only appreciated long after they'd reached the top. Another such example is the album you are holding now. As far as anyone knows, this is the very first production of Shania from the time that she still worked under her own name, Eilleen Edwards, in the Deerhurst Resort in Ontario.' The notes then go on to sketch Shania's career up to 1999.

The masters of these demo recordings were digitally mixed and re-mastered by veteran engineer Joe Venneri. A significant portion of the proceeds from the sale of this recording is being donated to the Make A Wish Foundation and Second Harvest/Kids' Café. Jomato Records representative Mark Saxon states that, 'We obtained the legal right to release the recordings throughout the world.' He went on to warn about the existence of bootleg versions: 'There are a few on the market,' he explained. 'Our authentic release has twelve tracks on it. Some bootlegs have ten, some eleven, some twelve. All of the bootlegs we've encountered so far with less than twelve were made off of an early, unmastered demo we had. They are lacking about 35 per cent of the music – all of the overdubs that were on the master – and they're fourth generation or worse, made from a cassette copy.' Information about the session, as it exists, explained Saxon, is sketchy. 'The musicians list is as complete as we have records on, we're missing a few, but here's what we have listed: Eilleen Twain – lead and backing vocals, Paul Sabu – guitars, backing vocals, Ray Naccari – keyboards, Rick Howard – guitars, Kevin St Claire – bass, John Wanzling – drums, percussion. It was recorded in Canada during 1989 and 1990. It [the session] was produced by Harry Hinde with Paul Sabu.'

Listening to the CD it is clear that Shania was not fooling when she spoke about rock music being her thing. Fans of the Shania Twain who bought *The Woman In Me* and *Come On Over* are likely to be somewhat disappointed by this album. There is only the faintest hint of the singer who would conquer the world with her sophisticated and intricately constructed style a mere five years

later. For the most part the songs on this album are wholly unremarkable AOR. The 'mix' serves to bring Eilleen's voice (often hard, sometimes harsh, never soft) out of the mass of thumping drums, muddy bass, swirling cheap synthesizers and hysterical axe-grinding that so typified such mid-1980s poodle rock. The melodies are rather clichéd, the lyrical imagery astoundingly poor (witness the chorus to 'L.U.V. Eyes'). When the CD was released in the UK (licensed through producer Joe Veneri's Planet Nashville), it bore the title of track two, 'Wild & Wicked', a song remarkable only for its musical clichés (though it is nowhere as near as bad as the inane 'The Rhythm Made Me Do It' – which has a chorus that involves explaining to a cop . . . you can guess the rest).

Had Eilleen Twain never become famous, there's no doubt that this album would never have been allowed valuable racking space in music stores across the globe. All tracks are co-credited to Paul Sabu (except 'Half-Breed', of course, and 'For The Love Of Him'). On the sleeve to the American copy of the CD Sabu writes 'A Few Reminiscences', as they're labelled. 'Everything started with a simple phone call from Canadian producer Harry Hinde,' writes Sabu. The notes continue, 'He had discovered a new act, already had interest from A&M, and needed some songs. I had had success writing for another Canadian artist, Lee Aaron, so I got the call. Eilleen was performing in a cabaret show a few hours north of Toronto (brutally cold at that time of the year). Harry and Eilleen met me at the airport and we drove to the Deerhurst Country Club Resort. During the next few weeks, we got to know each other and started writing together. She had very recently lost her parents in a car accident and conversations about that resulted in our first co-write, "Send It With Love". That broke the ice and soon we had an album's worth of material.'

Explaining the recording process Sabu writes, 'Problem was, there were no studios in the area to record the material. Fortunately, the bass player had a small eight-track and we set up in his living room to record the instruments. The vocals were then added, with Eilleen singing from the only room we could isolate her in – the sauna!'

Sabu goes on to praise Eilleen's dedication to the project, her attitude, professionalism and her ability to persuade people to help in the making of the recordings. He ends his notes by stating that 'The time I spent with Eilleen was special to me. She was, and I suppose still is, a kind, sweet, gracious and thankful woman with a relentless will to succeed, which has obviously paid off. I'm proud to have shared some "first steps" with her.'

Apart from the previously mentioned 'Half-Breed', *Beginnings* offers no real suggestion as to Eilleen's mindset and points to an obviously rock-based direction at the time. The sleeve notes to *Beginnings* state that 'The recordings were made . . . deals were sought . . . but nothing really worked out for Shania and Limelight [Harry Hinde's company], so they parted company in 1990.' It was another false start for Eilleen. She was still starring in the review show at Deerhurst and earning warm applause, but it was coming from people who had turned up to see a professional show, expecting to be entertained certainly, but they hadn't paid to see and hear her alone; they were just there for the show. Which wasn't to devalue their applause, it was just that Eilleen had been reared to expect more than that. Her mother had always wanted her to be the centrepiece of any performance, to be the star of the show. Appearing in such a high-energy, professional stage show had helped Eilleen to learn valuable stagecraft for which she would always be grateful, but she wasn't developing her own songs or her solo career in any meaningful way. It must have been increasingly frustrating to her.

Eilleen had worked on the *Beginnings* songs on her days off, before shows, after shows and whenever she could. She'd begged and borrowed equipment that had to be carried through the snow and ice to a small hotel room at the resort and then she'd had to record in the bathroom! And it had all been for nothing. Rock music was just as difficult to crack as country, and she didn't like it as much. So it was then that Eilleen decided the time was right to re-embrace country music and try, once more, to conquer Nashville.

By the end of that year, 1990, Darryl and Mark were old enough to drive, to leave home and look after themselves. Eilleen was through with being a Mom during the day and a rock singer or showgirl at night. She could become something else now. So she called Mary Bailey again.

CHAPTER FOUR

THAT DON'T IMPRESS ME MUCH

Eileen was free – free from parental responsibilities and ready to face her own challenge – but was she good enough to make it in the music business? Her friend Mary Bailey had been close at hand all this time and she was convinced that Eileen had everything it took to become a star. She invested her own money in Twain and once again became her active manager. The direction they'd take, however, was all Shania's. Maybe the experience with Paul Sabu had something to do with it, but now Eileen was adamant. 'I always loved country music. The emotion, the music, it was what I had grown up on. I wanted to sing country music, and while I would always enjoy pop and rock it was country where I felt my roots were and where my own songs that I was writing were taking shape.'

So, of course, there was only one place to go. Nashville, Tennessee, or as it calls itself, Music City USA, the spiritual and financial home of country music since the 1920s. Nashville is to country music what Hollywood is to films. They are the factory, there the product is made, the myths created and most importantly, the Dream is made flesh – or rather, celluloid and whatever CDs are made of. The stars of Nashville, though, are generally of a particular type, that type having been invented more than sixty years ago and only occasionally re-drawn to suit the modern world. By the time that Eileen Twain was to make her third assault on the city the type had recently been amended to take in a rock-tinged edge, but it still didn't include being born anywhere north of the border.

Founded in 1780 as Nashborough and named after General Nash of North Carolina, Nashville has not always been keen to identify itself with country music. Especially since it was, after all, originally hillbilly music – 'music' that peasants from the Appalachian Mountains would play while they got drunk and carried on in all manner of godforsaken ways. Nashville has always been big on God. In fact, the biggest business in Nashville isn't actually country music at all, it is the printing of the Bible. It is easy to understand why the city's elders always had a higher view of

their home, the self-proclaimed 'buckle on America's Bible-belt'. The city's leaders of commerce and council like to refer to their city as the Athens of the South. They can point out to strangers the exact replica of the Parthenon (without the missing bits) built in the middle of the city's Centennial Park and the Nobel Prize-winning Vanderbilt University. It has been a thriving industrial centre, too, for quite a while; in the 1980s Nashville was home to more than ten per cent of the total Japanese investment in America, with Nissan being one of the biggest employers in an area at the city's limits.

The country music fraternity was originally lured to the city by a radio show which specialized in broadcasting 'mountain music' live to the southern states. Started in 1925 by George Dewey Hay, a regular Saturday-night 'hoe-down' broadcast on WSM (the *WSM Barn Dance*) brought crowds of mountain folk and their families to the city to play, sing, dance and get drunk. It is little wonder the god-fearing, teetotal moral majority of the city despised country music so much. And it could have been so different. Hay had been rejected in his attempts to broadcast his favourite style of music 150 miles (240km) south in Memphis for much the same reasons that Nashville's gentle folk would grow to hate it.

The country scene really came of age, though, in 1943 when the regular Saturday-night broadcast, which had changed its name to *The Grand Ol' Opry* in 1927, was beamed live from Nashville's Ryman Auditorium in the centre of downtown. The Ryman, an old, wooden-seated theatre with a wide, deep stage whose back door opened on to a bar (naturally kept regularly oiled and used by many a star), would prove to be a Mecca for country music fans from around the world for the next sixty years. It is still visited today, despite it no longer being used for the Opry broadcasts – they moved to a massive, specially built complex with a hotel and theme park on the city's fringes, in 1974.

Traditionally, mountain folk from the Appalachians have been close-knit, conservative and suspicious of outsiders. The country music scene that grew up in Nashville adopted many Appalachian ways; it has never been a place where outsiders have been treated warmly, especially if they dare to think they can sing country music. When Australian Olivia Newton-John won a Female Vocalist award at the Country Music Association Awards in the 1970s, a gang of older stars, including husband and wife team George Jones and Tammy Wynette, boycotted the event, claiming that a foreigner could not be called country. Ten years later things hadn't changed much when another Canadian female with a deep love of country music attempted to make it there. Of course, not only did kd lang have her nationality against her; she was also ironic (not a big draw in Nashville), sported a mid-1950s-style Elvis Presley quiff and was quite possibly gay!

What had drawn kd to Music City, USA was her love of both Patsy Cline and the only Canadian country singer to make it there, Anne Murray. Like Shania after her, kd would try to

win the approval of Nashville's policy makers and bosses by working with old-time country giants – in her case ex-Cline producer Owen Bradley on her second album (but first Nashville recording) *Shadowland*, a beautiful collection of classic 1950s country torch songs by the likes of Ernest Tubbs, Roger Miller and Harlan Howard/Billy Walker. She even got three of Nashville's biggest old-style female stars to back her vocally on the fabulous 'Honky Tonk Angels Medley' – Kitty Wells, Brenda Lee and Loretta Lynn. The ploy worked for kd up to a point: she got to play at the CMA Awards in 1988 and her follow-up album *Absolute Torch And Twang* received a fair amount of country music airplay, but she was never really accepted or trusted by Nashville's self-appointed moral conscience. Even when in 1991 she scored a massive worldwide hit with the album that really crossed over to the pop audience, *Ingenue*, Nashville still said that she wasn't 'one of them'. When the worldwide tour to support the multi-million-selling album ended after more than a year, kd upped and moved to LA. She rarely went back.

At the time that kd went to Tennessee, country music was only just beginning to claw back some of the popularity it had lost during the late 1970s when a bland, string-laden Nashville Sound favoured by the pre-eminent producers of the day (take a bow, Chet Atkins) had taken all the originality out of the genre. The 'Outlaw' breed of Willie Nelson, Waylon Jennings, Merle Haggard, Jerry Jeff Walker *et al* had pretty much been the only interesting thing in town, which is not to denigrate The Mandrells, George Hamilton IV or Conway Twitty, but really, each release of theirs could be counted on to be pretty darned similar to the last. In the mid-1980s Dolly Parton and Kenny Rogers were the hottest things around, and that was because they'd stepped outside the strict parameters of country music to sell to pop fans. Nashville needed something new.

By the time Eileen Twain decided that Nashville would be her ultimate destination the country music scene had indeed found something new and had been truly revolutionized by a plump farmer's boy from Oklahoma with a marketing degree. In 1989 Garth Brooks had begun a sales assault with his first two albums, *Garth Brooks* and *No Fences*, which would, by 1992, result in his selling over thirty million albums worldwide. This was more than Michael Jackson and Madonna, previously the world's biggest-selling album artists, had managed in the same period.

By then, the whole of America's music industry had decided that Nashville was where they ought to be. Major record labels who had previously had offices only on each coast began to open up major operations in the quaint, two-storey houses which made up Nashville's Music Row. New acts and old were being regularly launched and relaunched in the style of Garth; big hats were in for the men, hair was more natural for the women, though still high (as kd lang said, 'the higher the hair, the closer to God'). The music was also changing. Gone were the strings and weeping pedal-steel guitars. In came big drums and guitar solos. Garth Brooks was a big Billy Joel fan.

Live shows also changed dramatically. Garth flew – literally – on a wire above his audience's heads at gigs. He employed pyrotechnics, used a headset microphone and radio-microphone guitar so that he could run, leap and dance as only rock stars had before. Female stars like Wynonna Judd, previously the younger part of the hugely successful mother and daughter team The Judds, and Reba McIntire (who dared to be publicly divorced in Nashville) made sassy, almost feminist statements in their songs and videos. The world was in love with country music, and moreover, it was a country music that Eilleen Twain could relate to; it rocked.

Not that it was going to be easy. Just, perhaps, a little easier now that Nashville would accept rockers as country performers. Even though an outsider to Music City, Shania felt she had plenty to offer. 'Coming from Canada gives me an international outlook. We are exposed to all sorts of viewpoints and styles of music in Canada. I have always thought of myself as an international artist, not simply tied to any one format. I figure that that side of me would be great for Nashville since the industry has been attempting to break through internationally with its artists.'

Mary Bailey paid for Twain to make a demo tape of her voice and songs and she sent it to a friend of a friend of a friend, a high-powered Nashville attorney named Dick Frank. An eminent entertainment lawyer, Frank represented several heavyweight country artists and, given the 'everyone knows everyone else' nature of Nashville, had found record deals for several new acts over the years. He liked to think he knew talent when he saw it and was clued in to how things were going in Nashville. He'd seen the new guys coming into his business looking for something other than the backwoods girls with hay in their hair and a twang in their voice. He must have heard the rock element in Eilleen's demo and looked at the attractive woman in the photos sent by Bailey, and seen something of the future. He headed to Deerhurst to watch Eilleen Twain in action.

Frank was impressed by the vivacious performance and distinctive vocal style. He told everyone he would do what he could and on return to Nashville went to work. In an echo of kd lang's first attempts to woo the Nashville establishment. an old-style, well-regarded producer named Norro Wilson was impressed enough by the demo tape and descriptions of Shania's on-stage talents to want to pursue matters. Later, when Eilleen's first Nashville-produced album was finished, the old-school element of the package would prove to be a negative factor, but at that time the fact that someone so experienced and with great contacts in the business was willing to work with her was a bonus. It could only help to open doors which had previously been resolutely locked to her.

Wilson invited Twain to Nashville to make some recordings. No promises, no record deals, just the opportunity to test her voice, try out some material and see if she had what it takes. Talent spotters in Nashville are offered outstanding music demo tapes every day, but nine times out of ten the artist or wannabe artist in question has little or no stage presence. This can result in delays in the making of a star while that act is taken on the road to learn the craft. Ironically, while

49

Nashville would come to think of Twain as primarily a studio creation, she initially won interest and attention thanks to her professional and dynamic stagecraft.

Almost a novice in the studio and somewhat daunted by the speed of recording, Twain took a little time to find her voice, but Wilson was pleased enough with the final results to play the tape to a friend at Mercury Records. He immediately recommended the young Canadian to label head Harold Shedd. Another veteran of the industry, Shedd had not been in the job long and so was looking to make his mark. Mercury had been successful but had slipped of late and it was his job to bring success. He had previously discovered Alabama, a southern boogie-based country band who went on to be one of the biggest-selling country music groups in history. At that time, Shedd was on a roll; he'd just finished work on the debut album of Billy Ray Cyrus who had just rocked the country world with the catchy 'Achy Breaky Heart' – a song which was to play a major part in Eilleen Twain's future. Shedd agreed to sign Twain to Mercury Records on one condition. The record business veteran just could not see Eilleen Twain working as a name for a modern country music star. Eilleen was prepared to change her first name but there was no way she could ever lose her father's name, so she thought hard about an alternative to Eilleen. She remembered the girl from Deerhurst called Shania, and so it began. Shania had a cool sound and a pertinent meaning.

There seemed to be no time between the deal being offered and Shania being in the studio. Press releases went out from Mercury Records about this new, young star, avoiding too much about her being Canadian lest it prove a barrier to some of the more conservative elements of the media. Photo shoots, media training, everything a starlet needed was set up around her studio dates. 'It was an amazing time,' Shania told me in 1995. 'It was a dream come true, but it all happened so fast. People were so nice and welcoming.' But there was one thing bothering the always focused and determined Shania. The record label did not want her to record her own songs. In a surprisingly backward-looking move, the experienced producer decided that Shania should rely on the songwriting skills of the thousands of songwriters who populate Music Row rather than chance her own rockier, sassy numbers. Mercury, in the shape of Harold Shedd who co-produced the album along with Norro Wilson, wanted Shania to have the best chance possible, as they saw it, of scoring a hit record. And the surest way that they knew to do that was to go to tried and trusted writers for material. Which on the face of it was odd, since presumably they had taken a chance on her because she was a future star like the people making waves then in Nashville – the rockier songwriters who had attitude. But instead of letting her go straight out with her own stuff, they argued, she should get established, then she could start recording original material. (Of course, in retrospect it looks as if they had been right all along.)

Shania was not happy, but naturally, she must have reasoned, these guys knew far more than she did – so she went along with the plan. 'I understood,' she said later of the decision, 'but

something worried me about it. I knew my songs were good and that I'd perform my own material much better than anyone else's. But I had no power at that point, I was a new artist about to work on a debut album.'

So, not for the first time, but almost certainly for the last, Eilleen settled down to do just what she was told because it was good for her. Except, crucially, this time she wasn't Eilleen. It would take some time for the full realization to sink in, of the scope being offered to her to change, but Eilleen was now Shania. And as Shania she had to be someone special, someone if possible who could be fantastic for the PR department – which would, in turn, mean her being someone else for the world at large. Writing her press releases and starting a fan club taught Eilleen a lot about the music business which she hadn't previously known. Meeting strangers in strange places and remembering to answer to a strange name could have been unsettling at first, possibly even disorientating. But Shania had to get used to it, and fast. Just as she had done when she was a small child, Eilleen was singing other people's country songs, pretending to be someone else. The big difference now, though, was that Eilleen had invented that someone else and she was beginning to understand how useful the someone else could be. As Shania she could, and would, develop the persona to protect Eilleen from the world that had, thus far, treated her so cruelly. Not straight away – it would take time and the intervention of someone in her life who could offer the kind of advice and protection she craved – but soon Shania Twain would be the world's favourite country/pop creation.

CHAPTER FIVE

DON'T BE STUPID

Contradictions occur in everyone's life. Sometimes they come along a bundle at a time. For Shania, the making and release of her eponymous debut album was such a time. She'd been signed to a major label presumably because she had the makings of a star. At that time everyone was looking for a certain formula in both male and female stars (as they always do in Nashville), which meant being able to rock, having an attitude not unlike Wynonna or Reba or even the more laid-back Trisha Yearwood who was just breaking through – all tumbling locks, sombre face and Garth Brooks-penned tunes. Yet here was Shania singing other people's songs that made her out to be a clichéd little lady, unlucky in love, standing by her man – see Mike Reid and Kent Robbins's 'When He Leaves You', which casts the singer as a frequently cheated-on wife, advising her husband's soon-to-be-ex-girlfriend that he always does this and still comes home to her. Seven of the ten songs on her debut release were written or co-written by men and only three were new at the time of recording.

Shania was happy with the recording process on that first release (the recordings which comprised *Beginnings/Wild & Wicked* would not be released commercially until after Shania had achieved international fame), but was confused as to why the company would not allow her more than one of her own compositions on it. The one number which did make it, 'God Ain't Gonna Getcha For That', is by far the most original and striking song on the release. It's also the odd one out, of course, in so far as the singer is definitely female and yet dares to take the lead in talking to a stranger in a bar, offering to buy him a drink and even (gasp!) take him for a drive, and then goes on to say that God would not punish the stranger for going. Maybe it was something to do with the fact that she was surrounded by men old enough to be her father (or at least uncle), but none of them seemed to understand what she wanted to do. They had been smart enough to realize that the world was ready for her when they signed her, so why couldn't they let the world see her as she really was, or wanted to be?

Corbis

55

Of course, for Shedd and Wilson the world was changing; they just didn't get how fast. It must have come as something of a shock when Billy Ray Cyrus's saccharine-sweet, simple, catchy and corny 'Achy Breaky Heart' made unprecedented million-plus sales around the world, even in the UK – a market so hard to break that acts as big as Dolly and Kenny still had to plan pan-European tours in order to make a profit. Unfortunately for Shania, the success of the cartoon-country 'Achy Breaky Heart' can only have served to reinforce her bosses' view that country was still where it was at.

Shedd and Wilson did allow a bit of rock and roll into Shania's first record, in the shape of Rachel Newman's 'Got A Hold On Me', but in retrospect they must have realized what a mistake it was to do so. While the rest of *Shania Twain* is at least crystal-clear and sparklingly bright, 'Got A Hold On Me' is muddy and indistinct – in fact it sounds like an outtake from those earlier Paul Sabu recordings.

In a final act of contradiction the album sleeve artwork was designed to emphasize, rather than ignore, Shania's Canadian background. The photo shoot for the cover was even conducted in Timmins! Of course, that might have been because Shania told Mercury that she could get good rates for the shoot crew, although even more money could have been saved by making the decision to photograph her accompanied by a tame wolf in a studio made to look like a field of snow. Regardless of that, the choice of cover co-star and outfit – buckskin, fur-trimmed jacket, boots and blue jeans for the front, native craft earrings, big hair and native-style blanket jacket for the back – seemed designed to tell the world that this woman was from the far, frozen north. And they don't get many wolves in Chicago.

Upon release, *Shania Twain* did not exactly set the world alight. Shania felt trapped. She had everything in the world she wanted except what she desperately needed: more control. The self-titled debut album sold some, but Shania was unhappy. She knew why it had not been the success she craved; as she explained, 'It wasn't me; I was just a singer on that album. I had no real input.'

However, from the singing point of view, it should have served to win favour with critics who would later cast doubt on her ability to perform live, suggesting, as they did, that her voice was not up to the rigours of live work. Listening to *Shania Twain* makes it difficult to understand such Nashville-based critics of Shania's vocal skills, since they must have heard this album (or at least should have heard it). It ably showcases her country-style vocals. The album is more country than her later work, which should have made purists happy, and the material shows her ability to mix a pop style with a country inflection, notably on the song 'Forget Me'. In fact, as a standard-fare country album of the late 1980s/early 1990s, it holds up pretty well. It may lack the hit songs of her later works, but for a debut it won solid reviews in the USA and around the world (the first clue that Shania would have international appeal). It also included, of course, her first single

release, the upbeat, fizzy 'What Made You Say That?' which, despite not being a hit (reaching only the fifties on America's *Billboard* chart), did at least open new doors for her elsewhere. Very important doors, at that.

'What Made You Say That?' was released to radio, but with country music exploding at the time it was an enormous battle for Mercury Records to gain serious airtime on the powerful, consortium-owned, major-market radio stations. With Garth, Reba, Randy Travis, Clint Black and the rest ruling the airwaves it was tough work to break a new act stateside. The single, although it did chart, was a long way from being a smash. But Shania had something going for her that most of her competitors were missing.

Ten years previously pop and rock music had been revolutionized by MTV and the video age, but country music, as ever, was still behind in the video revolution. It had its own twenty-four-hour video channel, Country Music Television (CMT), but the videos it displayed lacked the excitement and visual creativity of their rock and pop cousins. Mercury had already seen just how photogenic Shania was from her publicity photo shoots and decided it was worth investing serious money in a video. In another of those contradictory moves that had so far typified her time at the label, they sent her and a crew to Miami and came back with a video controversy that was significant in establishing her name, at least.

Maybe the decision to film Shania on the beach was more than just cynical exploitation of a pretty girl taking off some of her clothing. Or maybe not. Maybe it was their way of saying 'sorry' for making her shoot the album cover in below-freezing snow in the decidedly un-glamorous location of Timmins. Whatever the reason, the result was certainly powerful. Shania cavorting in the sand and exposing her navel sent shockwaves through the traditionally conservative country music establishment.

It was bizarre. Mercury had forced her into making a safe, unremarkable album of standard-fare country songs and packaged it with photographs of her as a bouffant-haired, fully-made-up, pretty but nothing special Nashville girl singer, and yet, for her first single release they helped her to make a decidedly unusual-for-country music video. At least Shania was beginning to make a name for herself, though. People were looking, if not listening.

The video won attention for her and even an award in Europe as most promising newcomer (the Rising Star Award) at CMT Europe. But she was still a nobody in terms of record sales and the all-important airplay needed in order to sell huge quantities of records in America. So Mercury decided that she should go and meet her potential audience in person. Now the usual way to break in a new act on the road is to buy them on to a major tour with a big artist, booking the newcomer as show opener. That way at least audiences are guaranteed to see the newcomer – at least those members of the audience who arrive in the auditorium in time to see an opening act. Plus, of course, the fact that the newcomer had toured with a big name won them credibility points and a degree of recognition among the public as the act who toured with Garth/Reba/Randy/George etc.

However, Mercury, in their wisdom, decided to break a few rules with Shania and instead sent her on the road on a newcomer triple-header with Tony Keith and John Brennan. Shania was used to playing live, but not touring for so long. As she tellingly wrote in her first ever open letter to members of her fan club, which had been established on the release of *Shania Twain*, 'The fans make all the travelling and loneliness worth it.' Shania found life on the road in a shared bus and shared band hard. It wasn't helped, of course, by the fact that she had to perform songs from her album, none of which she particularly liked apart from 'God Ain't Gonna Getcha For That'. As the tour rolled across the mid-west, Tony Keith, who was old-time country, did quite well from the exposure, but Shania did not impress. Remembering that period Shania recalls, 'I just knew I could do better with my own songs. It was not working the other way – I wasn't feeling that I was being myself on stage. I wanted more.' Shania had become, finally, sick of waiting – of not getting her own way. As she told a British newspaper in 1999 when asked what she would change about herself, 'I would want to be more patient. I get so agitated.' Her patience was being sorely tested, but things were about to give. And give big.

Because of the mainly judgemental and critical attention the video garnered in the US, Shania was being seen as different from the pack. The video's success on CMT also led to phone calls from two most unlikely characters. Sean Penn, long out of his marriage to Madonna, had previously stayed in Nashville for a while on a location shoot and had taken to country music. Watching CMT one day he saw the debuting Shania and was immediately on the phone to the label suggesting he direct her next project. Shania was naturally pleased, if a little taken aback. Mercury were more than happy for them to work together. The next single was destined to be 'Dance With The One That Brought You'. Penn duly directed, bringing along with him veteran Hollywood actor Charles Durning.

It was one of the classiest and sweetest videos Shania would make. Significantly. Once again, because of a well-made video, Shania was beginning to set herself apart from the rest of the crowd. She was a little controversial and was attracting the attention of Hollywood and those outside Nashville. Most people would have thought that she was definitely on to something here. With the benefit of hindsight, of course, as any fool knows, it was obvious Shania was destined to become a star. And yet, and yet . . .

At the time Mercury were happy neither with the sales of the first two singles nor those of the debut album. Her videos had caused a storm of controversy, but that had not translated into cash on the barrel for them; it had not translated into album sales. No one seemed to think that this might be because there was a certain amount of incongruity between what they saw on screen and what they heard on the CD – if they heard it, because radio still had not begun rotating any of it. Sexy poses and a bare navel do not sell as well over the airwaves as they do on TV. By May 1993, almost a year on from the beginning of the recording process for the album, the point when Eilleen truly thought that her life was about to change and that her mother's dream for her was to be realized, it looked as if it might easily be slipping away from her.

And then one night Shania took another phone call that was truly to change her life. This time, though, the voice on the other end was not familiar to her and the news was not at all bad.

60

Shania steps out in
public with her
husband three paces
behind her. Mutt
attempts to avoid
the limelight.

CHAPTER SIX

YOU WIN MY LOVE

By the beginning of 1993, Country Music Television had branched out into international waters. CMT Europe was the main thrust of the attack and was proving a small success with audiences from England to Czechoslovakia. Suddenly it seemed that country music's new youthful image was becoming clear to people who still perceived Nashville as being all about having big hair and wearing sequins.

This was very good news for Shania. Her career may have been slow to develop in the US, but in Europe, where country music fans preferred a little more spice in their mix, Shania was becoming a star. Head of Programming for CMT Europe, Cecilia Walker recalls that 'whenever we played Shania's videos we were immediately inundated with hundreds of letters from fans thanking us and from viewers wanting to know more about her, if they were unfamiliar with her work. She had everything for the European market. She looked good, she had country married to pop and rock, which appealed to the audience there who were not so keen on traditional country, and most significantly she was cool. England in particular embraced Shania because she seemed to be sassy and hip. She was a very important part of CMT Europe's early success and she was rightly named International Star in 1995.'

Early that year (1993), so the legend goes, in a recording studio in England, rock producer Robert John 'Mutt' Lange was watching CMT, as was his wont – probably with the sound turned down. Lange was a man used to getting his own way, and rightly so, since he was arguably the most successful rock record producer in the world at that time. His credits included making international stars out of Australian heavy rockers AC/DC, American former new wave band The Cars (he produced their multi-million-selling breakthrough single, 'Drive'), British soft metal megastars Def Leppard, Foreigner and Canadian rocker Bryan Adams, among others. That particular day Lange was mixing a Bryan Adams album presciently titled *So Far So Good*. If anyone objected to having CMT on in the background, they didn't mention it. Lange was apparently a heavy-duty country music fan who bought all the new releases and grew up as a big fan of classic country as well – one former bandmate from the mid-1970s claims that as a kid, while his classmates rocked to Elvis, Mutt swayed along with Slim Whitman. This was either an incredibly brave thing to do or is an entirely apocryphal tale. Whatever the case, between knob-twiddling, Lange would appreciate the sights on CMT. That day, like many others before and plenty after, Shania Twain's debut video appearance, with its navel flaunting and seaside cavorting, caught his attention and he became transfixed. Maybe, if the info on screen at the end of the video had mentioned her nationality, he might have asked Adams if her knew her (as it happens, he did not). Lange sent someone out to find the CD. Eventually Lange got a copy of *Shania Twain* and he listened hard.

Now, clearly, Lange was attracted by the singer's sultry looks, but just as clearly he heard something in her voice, something that just as clearly Shania's bosses at Mercury had heard, too, even if they did not know how to realize it in her. Later Lange would tell her she had hit potential (as if she didn't already know) and that he knew how to make something of it. But for now he had to make contact with her.

As previously stated, Lange likes to have things his own way. Not that he shouts or screams or throws tantrums. Quite the opposite, it seems. According to Def Leppard's Phil Collen he's 'The most easy-going dictator you'll ever meet', and Bryan Adams says that, 'When tension starts to build [in the studio] we just let it blow.' Lange has always worked slowly and meticulously with his acts, building the songs piece by piece, bar by bar. Meatloaf co-writer and producer Jim Steinman said of him, 'Mutt's like Frankenstein, he pieces little bits of skin together,' adding, to make clear that this was not meant as an insult, 'I'm a big fan of the guy, I think he's one of the most brilliant producers in the world.' So the reason that Lange was watching CMT that day as opposed to MTV (or no TV at all) may well have been because he just loved country music, or it may have been something different.

For most of the 1980s, rock music – the kind that Mutt Lange made – had ruled the world. The albums he produced, from 1980's *Back In Black* by AC/DC, through the same band's *For Those About To Rock*, taking in Foreigner's *4* and *Records*, Def Leppard's *High 'N' Dry*, *Pyromania* and *Hysteria* and not forgetting The Cars' *Heartbeat City* (including 'Drive') were the major-selling albums of their time. Only Michael Jackson and Madonna had surpassed sales figures of Lange acts, and he had even, as if to prove that he could do that too, worked with Billy Ocean on the singer's massive *Tear Down These Walls* in 1988. Yet in the 1990s rock music sales had begun to be overtaken by those of Garth Brooks, a country act. Sure, Lange's relationship with Adams had produced huge sales, including the massive single 'Everything I Do (I Do It For You)', but he must have been intrigued by the growth in popularity of the country market after Garth had arrived on the scene in 1990. So, while he may well have been a fan of country music, by 1993 everyone working in music had to be. Maybe, just maybe, Mutt Lange was looking for a way to get a piece of that action. And what better way to do it than to create a female Garth? That would be a sexy proposition and, apart from Tina Turner – whom he was booked to work with in 1993 – Mutt had not worked with a big female star before.

Mutt Lange (front row, at right) with members of his first band Hocus in 1971.

Despite being such a big name in record production, or perhaps because of it, Mutt Lange had remained a fairly low-key figure. But then again, what does anyone know about any other rock record producers? It has become part of the legend since he and Shania have become an item that Lange liked to keep it that way. But it had not always been the case. During the first half of the 1970s Mutt had been in a couple of bands, singing and playing guitar with Hocus in his native South Africa in 1970–71 – the name no doubt derived from the then-popular Dutch muso band Focus's big hit, 'Hocus Pocus' – and doing the same in London with the Arthur Brown Band. Which must have been odd: Brown was the madman who in 1967 released, as The Crazy World of Arthur Brown, the hit single 'Fire', which he would perform complete with a burning crown on his head.

According to Geoff Williams in South Africa, Lange was in 1970 already a sound engineer in a recording studio. As Williams explains, 'Mutt spent most of his childhood years in a place called Mufilira in the Copper Belt region of Northern Rhodesia (now Zimbabwe). His family moved down to South Africa when Mutt was a teenager. He completed his schooling in the little town of Belfast. He has two brothers, namely Bill (known as 'Slug') and Peter.

Another former schoolpal of Lange's, Johan du Pooy, fills in further details about his childhood. 'We were both at Guinea Fowl High School outside Gwelo, where we played in the same cricket team. He was the opening bowler in our team as he had a fast delivery. After two

years there we both were sent by our parents to complete our high schooling in South Africa at Belfast High School. It took us about two days by train to get to boarding school from Zimbabwe to South Africa. There he developed his interest in guitar playing and did sing a bit but not always on key! Throughout his high school days he was always quiet and reserved but not withdrawn.'

Du Pooy continues, 'Several of us formed a rock band for a short while (I have no idea what we called ourselves any more) and our lead singer and lead guitarist (Roland Deal) went on to make a few records in South Africa and became a commercial artist. Mutt played rhythm and harmonized with Roland, [and] the two of them taught me to play a bass guitar as they needed one (I went on to complete medicine and later emigrated to Canada – I was and am still a useless musician) and the drummer (James Borthwick) I think ended up in the South African Broadcasting Corporation.'

He continues, 'Even back then he said he was going to produce records and write music and we all thought "Oh yeah, yeah." Little did we know how successful he would become . . . '

Geoff Williams picks up the tale of Lange's musical development. 'I was the drummer in Mutt's band Hocus in South Africa back in 1970–71. When I first met [him], he was a sound engineer at a recording studio/production house, where he was mostly involved in producing jingles for radio. Shortly thereafter, we both quit our day jobs to focus on the band and our music. We shared a house on a large plot of land on the outskirts of Johannesburg, which was close enough to the action of the city, yet quiet enough to rehearse without bugging the neighbours.

'We worked incredibly hard (driven by one Robert John 'Mutt' Lange – who else?) and were soon putting out quite a respectable sound. We played a lot of country rock in the early days (Mutt's Nashville critics, please note!) and some of our influences included The Byrds, Poco, Grateful Dead, Crosby Stills Nash and Young and others. At the same time, we were listening to and playing some British rock; there was this little guy just starting out named Elton John. There were also Emerson Lake and Palmer, Free, Rod Argent and King Crimson, to name but a few. We also played some original material and, with our very diverse, mixed bag of influences, I think I can say we put out quite a distinctive sound, which would be difficult to label or categorize.

'Mutt was very much a sound and balance man. In those days there were no synths or computer-aided music, nor any on-stage miking or mixing (certainly not in our neck of the woods). What you played was what you got! Mutt and I worked closely and kept bass and drums very tight, vocals and harmonies were clear and prominent, instrumentation was clear, uncluttered and complemented the overall effect of the song.

'Mutt was also a very talented vocalist with an enormous versatility. He had a voice which could roar, it could also whisper. His natural voice had a kind of a Van Morrison/John Fogerty quality. I can still hear Mutt's vocal influence strongly in the artists he produces today. Leppard, Adams and, more recently, Shania. They all share those little throaty and nasal intonations which were so much part of Mutt's own singing. A coincidence? I think not. I know they have the best coach in the business. You can be the judge.

'Sadly (for me, that is), Hocus split around the end of 1971 and Mutt got more involved in producing. He produced several local South African artists and notched up quite a few hits before packing his bags and heading for London and the big world out there. And the rest, as they say, is history. For me, I am very privileged to have been associated with Mutt and, without being overly dramatic, I know we are all witnessing a legend at work.'

By the time Lange reached England, he was in his mid-twenties and was obviously a very good sound man. In order to make a living he decided to seek work as a producer and immediately became known for a certain style of sound. His first album work was with City Boy (he produced their first three albums, the last of which in 1978 spawned a hit single in '5705'), Graham Parker (with whom he would continue to work on and off throughout his career), The Motors, The Rumour and Bob Geldof's Boomtown Rats (producing their first three albums – the really successful ones – *Boomtown Rats* [1977], *Tonic For The Troops* [1978] and *The Fine Art of Surfacing* [1979]). Mutt was England's premier new wave producer. He even worked with XTC.

Then he met AC/DC, like him ex-pats from a former British colony, in their case Australia. They had travelled to the UK to find fame and rock and roll fortune. Mutt would prove to have the stamps for their passports to fame, despite the fact that the band had a particularly silly gimmicky lead guitarist, Angus Young, whose stage gear consisted of a school uniform complete with cap, satchel and shorts. He would cut a particularly daft figure as, standing atop a massive speaker stack on the side of the stage when the band played live, he threw his right hand in the air in a devil's horn shape, shaking his shaggy head until the cap fell off. Surely Mutt must have issued a low giggle at such antics.

After producing AC/DC's multi-million-selling *Highway To Hell* album in 1979, he became the rock producer to have. His reputation was made and then cemented by work with Def Leppard and Foreigner. Thus, when Shania finally realized who this man with the strange accent was who was calling her, she really did 'love everything he'd made'.

Through industry contacts Lange tracked down Shania's manager Mary Bailey, who of course had no idea of his credentials. In that first interview I conducted with Shania, she positively glowed when telling the story of her meeting with Mutt Lange. 'My manager told me this guy in England had seen my video and was interested in me. I guessed he was a songwriter and so eventually I took a call from him. I didn't know who Mutt Lange was – I know that sounds crazy when you think of all that he has done from AC/DC to Def Leppard to Bryan Adams, but I really didn't know. We started talking and connected immediately. He loved country music, probably more than I did. He'd play songs to me down the phone and I'd tell him what I thought. It was fascinating. We started talking every day, for hours. Eventually I had enough courage to play him one of my songs. It was at a time when I wasn't confident with my material – the company hadn't let me record them. Amazingly to me, Mutt loved my songs and told me he couldn't understand why they weren't on the album. That comment gave me so much confidence, especially from a man who had written and produced so many hits. It was inspiring. We started writing songs down the telephone and just talking for hours. I was able to get to know Mutt in a very personal way long before we ever met in person.' No doubt during those phone calls Shania would have learned of Mutt's own near-death experience in a car crash just months before the one that would kill her parents. He was hospitalized for three months after a crash in late 1986.

Just as Shania was pumped up by the attention of an industry legend, so Mutt was intrigued by her. He talked his pal Bryan Adams into making a trip to Nashville with him. They went to Fan Fair in June 1993, ostensibly for a fun vacation – Adams recalls that he was asked onstage to duet with Billy Ray Cyrus on 'Achy Breaky Heart' and did not know the words – but Mutt was more interested in meeting Shania.

Fan Fair is exactly what it says. For one week in June the Tennessee State Fairgrounds at Nashville are opened up to country music fans from all over the world. Every day they get to see concerts and actually meet and greet their heroes. Lange went to see Shania's performance at the Mercury Records show (different labels book the stage on different days for their acts only). He was impressed. She was a new artist with little following, but he recognized talent when he saw it. He also knew he was drawn to this unusually determined but vulnerable woman. When they did meet as Shania recalls, it was special moment: 'I ran across and hugged him. And I don't do that kind of thing. But we'd talked so much it was like seeing an old friend. There was definitely some strange connection between us.' That connection was about to become incredibly strong and incredibly powerful.

67

68

CHAPTER SEVEN

THE WOMAN IN ME

Before any romance could develop between Shania and Mutt (though it seems that it had already begun on the phone), there was business to attend to. Mercury was not happy with Shania's commercial success and was, naturally, interested in talking with Lange about producing the next album. It has been suggested that chances are, if Lange had not shown interest in working with her, there would never have been a second Shania Twain album. He was new Mercury President Luke Lewis's first choice to produce her second project – if they could overcome one major problem. Country albums have never been as expensively made as rock albums, primarily because, with a few exceptions, country albums have never sold in the same quantities as rock albums. Also, Lange was known as a high-budget producer who spent months in the studio creating his masterpieces. Usually, country albums were turned around in a matter of weeks. But Luke Lewis was excited. Sandy Neese, Vice-President of Media for Mercury, recalls that 'everyone was kind of unsure about a rock producer coming in but we all knew Shania was different to the rest and there was this feeling that we could be on to something massive. Nobody quite imagined just how important that decision to have Mutt produce would be.'

Lange reportedly put $250,000 of his own money on the table if he could produce the next album. The label agreed. The result, of course, and much to everyone's relief, was a smash hit record, packed with hit singles. It quite simply changed the shape of country music. The album, *The Woman In Me*, would eventually sell over ten million copies.

The project took over a year to make and started with a songwriting trip to England, where Lange lived at that time. Shania wrote songs, picked up ideas and met her new friend's family. As they worked, that 'strange connection' between them was causing another reaction. As they put the framework to her second album together, Shania was falling in love. Just a few short months after they met at Fan Fair, Mutt flew Shania and family members to Paris and proposed. They married a couple of months later – at Deerhurst. This was the fairy tale romance to end them all.

71

At the wedding: (from left) Mark, Jill, Mutt, Shania, Carrie-Ann, Darryl.

A struggling survivor, about to lose her dream after initial failure on the main stage, suddenly falls in love and works with one of the most successful pop Svengalis in history. Such a story could only be possible in country music, or films. Speaking to me in the Nashville offices of Mercury Records to promote the release of *The Woman In Me*, Twain was effervescent, positively bubbling over with pride at the results of her collaboration with her husband. 'It's a country record with all kinds of influences. There's some kicking Cajun kinda fiddle all over it – and steel. Mutt loves steel guitar. People think he's this rock guy but he genuinely loves country music. I think the sound he has created, the overall sound, is gonna change country music. He has set new standards. And I like my voice now, he's found something that was missing before.'

Shania also demonstrated her global ambitions. 'I'm an international artist,' she said, having come to realize that stars like Mariah Carey and Whitney Houston sell records all over the world. She understood that, in turn, she would need to promote herself outside the US. Whenever she was in England visiting Mutt Lange's family she would make herself available to promotional outlets such as CMT. She was always ready to find time for press and radio interviews in Europe and quickly became a favourite new name among press and public alike.

Besides Shania's hard work promoting the album, the sound of *The Woman In Me* helped to shift Shania from lowly country singer to international idol. By Mutt's standards it was a quick record to make; it averaged a month per track. But what a difference a year in the studio with Mutt Lange makes. To begin with, the songs are all her and Mutt's work. Shania's clever way with words and attitude of a sassy, knowing woman combined with Mutt's encyclopedic knowledge of popular music to make songs which are very 'now' yet tinged with melodic remembrances of classics. From the first track echoing and updating the old cliché, 'Home Isn't Where The Heart Is Anymore', through to the gospel-tinged Billie Holiday-style 'God Bless The Child' (coincidentally the title of a Holiday ballad) which closed the record, the pedal steel guitars and close country harmonies draw in the country listener. The rock and pop fan can also hear in various songs hints of the music they have grown up with and loved: the Queen-like 'We Will Rock You' drum-beat middle eight in 'Any Man Of Mine' (which begins with the declaration 'This is what a woman wants . . . '); the Chuck Berry/Beach Boys-style classic car imagery of 'You Win My Love' (tellingly a Lange solo effort) full of '55 Chevys, Cadillacs and racing analogies; a Creedence Clearwater Revival-style swamp rock swagger to '(If You're Not In It For Love) I'm Outta Here'.

The album's first single, 'Whose Bed Have Your Boots Been Under', debuted in the *Billboard* charts in January 1995. The flip side followed and went to number one, the first of four consecutive such number ones for Shania from what would prove to be her breakthrough album. The hits were '(If You're Not In It For Love) I'm Outta Here', 'The Woman In Me', 'You Win My Love' and 'No One Needs To Know'. Two more singles followed in 1996, 'Home Ain't Where The Heart Is Anymore' and 'God Bless The Child', with proceeds going to the Kids' Café/Second Harvest Food Bank in the US. The album spent well over one hundred weeks on the charts, a phenomenal achievement for a new artist who had yet to begin her first national tour.

Perhaps predictably, so quick was Shania's success that the Nashville music industry was hesitant to accept her as one of their own. Shania was everywhere, CMT played her videos constantly, her image graced the covers of magazines everywhere and she was outselling almost all her competitors. She was named 1996's top country album artist by *Billboard* magazine. Her ten million-plus album sales for *The Woman In Me* won her the Academy of Country Music's Album of the Year Award: she was Favourite Female Country Artist at the American Music Awards. And at a time when long form music videos had all but stopped selling, her record company released *The Complete Woman In Me Video Collection*, which not surprisingly outsold all video collections that year. Prestigious magazines such as *Esquire* and *Newsweek* covered her story and she made debut appearances on the all-important taste-making TV talk shows, *Letterman* and *The Tonight Show* with Jay Leno.

The timing could not have been more perfect. Country music was still on the rise after the breakthrough Garth Brooks had made in the 1980s and Shania was perfectly suited to appeal to both country fans and the younger, recently discovered Spice Girls crowd. All she had to do was keep putting out catchy, radio-friendly songs and the sky was the limit. But just as she was soaring towards the firmament, an unexpected backlash began.

74

Cynical critics of the Nashville system could have foreseen it. Shania was an outsider and had dared to take country sales to a new level. Maybe Shania should have given kd lang a call to learn what she might expect next. The rumours started that she couldn't really sing, that Lange controlled the shots and she was nothing more than a puppet. The more popular she became the more Nashville knocked her. Country singer Steve Earle called her a high-paid lap dancer – as a former drug addict who had had his fair share of run-ins with the Nashville hierarchy (not to mention the law), perhaps he should have known better. Some of the more prudish, and possibly even hypocritical – since Nashville has always had more than its share of hypocrites (see Randall Reise's excellent *Nashville Babylon*, RGA Publishing Group, 1988) – said she flaunted her sexuality, her lyrics were trite and banal and the music bereft of any country soul. Most hurtfully, they claimed she was a phoney – she didn't sing live because she couldn't. Shania and Mutt had elected not to tour to support the release of *The Woman In Me*; perhaps Mutt wanted to ensure that the album stood or fell on its own merits, perhaps their schedule did not permit them to put together the kind of act that they would like. Whatever the reason, Shania did not tour, thus inviting criticism that she could not perform. Which of course was ludicrous. It was hurtful to Shania and made no sense. Two years earlier I had seen Shania sing in a small club in London. Accompanied by just a guitar player, her voice was perfect. A unique sound that was both powerful and vulnerable and totally suited to the quasi-feminist material she was writing.

Combined with such criticism, some country radio programmers balked at Shania's vaguely anti-male stance (as they saw it) and complained that 'Any Man Of Mine', the second single, sounded remarkably like 'a Def Leppard track'. It is difficult to know if that particular barb was more of an insult to Shania or Def Leppard. But, try as the country establishment might, they could not deny the record's sales. Essentially the snipes were the product of sheer envy. Nashville feared the outside influence of a rock producer like Mutt Lange coming in and changing the rules on them. Soon, went the simplistic logic, every artist would want to find their own rock Svengali and the Nashville system would be threatened.

Plus, of course, by not touring to support a new release by a relative unknown, she was really endangering the age-old system of promotion. By claiming she did not tour because she couldn't sing, the establishment was desperately trying to protect the unwritten rule that country music artists need to tour over 250 nights a year, as was the custom. Again a major part of the industry was being questioned and threatened. Millions of dollars change hands on live country tours; promoters, merchandizers, rigging contractors and jobbing musicians gained untold fortunes from servicing the live network that snaked out of Nashville. And Shania was to blame.

Garth Brooks had faced similar barbs a few years earlier, but worse was to come for Shania, something much more hurtful and personal. In April 1996, just as she was riding high, her birth father's family contacted Shania's hometown newspaper, the *Timmins Daily Press*. Essentially, Twain's biological grandmother accused Twain of not keeping in touch with her relatives. The paper took the opportunity to expand the story that Shania had 'invented' her native American heritage. Her grandmother was reported as saying, 'All she talks about is this Indian man, but what about her real father? What about us? I wrote about a year ago but once she started going good she never wrote. I wish she would. I don't know what's happened to her.'

Shania was upset, both on a personal level and as a professional matter. She did not want to be seen to be manipulating her heritage for publicity purposes. She took the bold step of countering the accusations with a statement to the *Timmins Daily Press*.

She said, 'I've never had a relationship with my biological father. From about the age of two years old, my mother and Clarence Edwards were separated. Soon after, Jerry assumed the role of

76

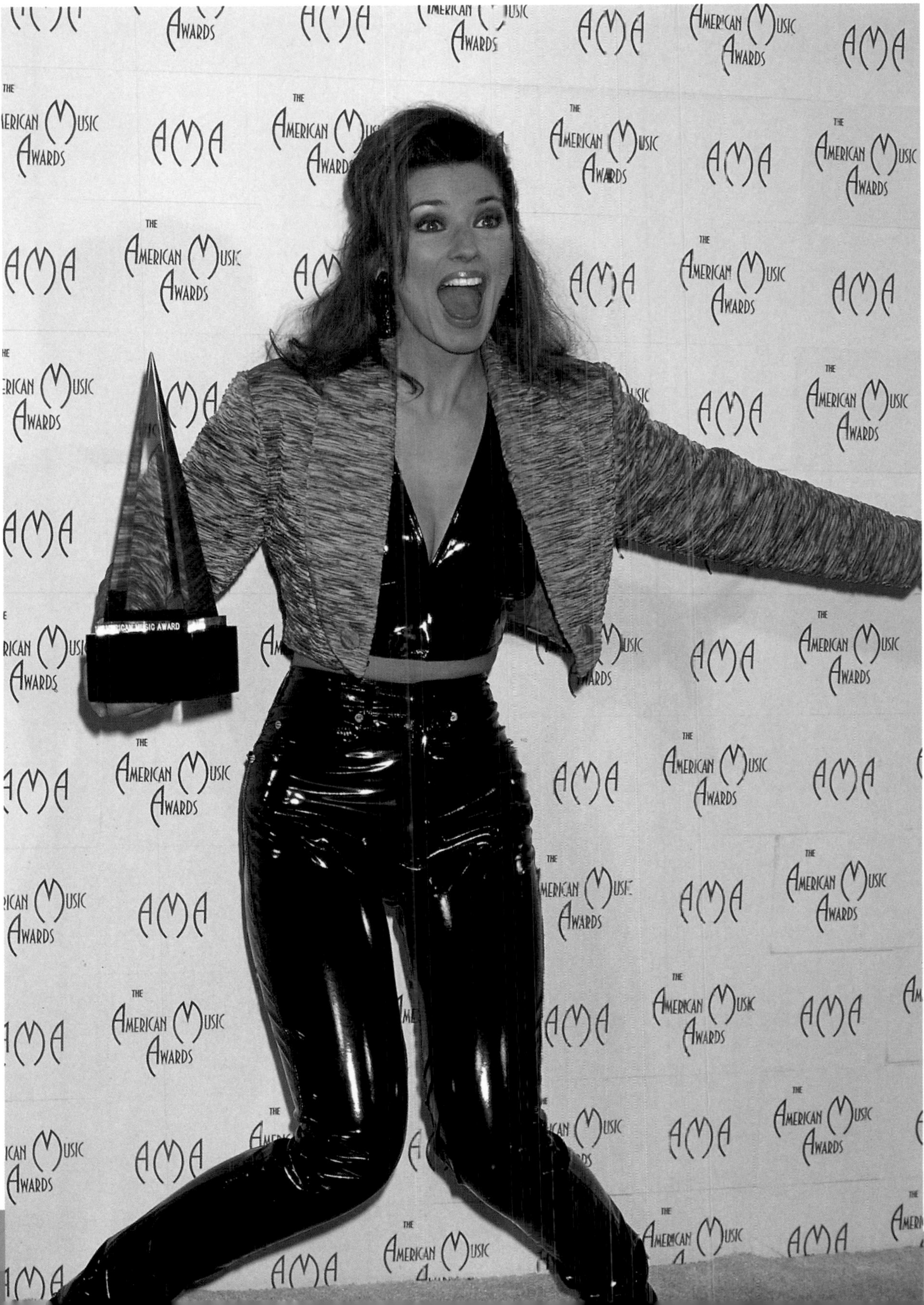

Pictorial/Jeffrey Mayer

being our father from that day forward even though it wasn't until a few years later that my mother and Clarence actually divorced and she and Jerry married. He was the only one who was there for me on a daily basis, through thick and thin until he died in 1987 in the car accident that also killed my mother.'

Her letter continued, 'I don't know how much Indian blood I actually have in me, but as the adopted daughter of my father Jerry, I became legally registered as fifty per cent North American Indian. Being raised by a full-blooded Indian and being part of his family and their culture from a young age is all I've ever known. That heritage is my heart and soul and I'm very proud of it.'

Talking to *Rolling Stone* magazine about the matter eighteen months later she said, 'The reality is that, to me, it's a very non-issue. Someone just took advantage of a situation to get some kind of recognition for it.' The reminder of the furore caused seemed to unsettle her. 'I'm very sensitive about a lot of things, actually,' she stated, going on to add, 'I'm sure that I come across as very driven, very direct, very focused and none of those things encompass my real sensitivity. But I'm a very sensitive person.'

One can only imagine how Shania was feeling. Or rather, how Eilleen was feeling. Shania was by now the front that helped Eilleen cope with the ravages of the world. Shania would brazenly front things out, but Eilleen was still smarting. Criticism hurt Eilleen, but it was directed at Shania, so that was kind of OK, wasn't it?. Even so, physical criticism is hard for anyone to handle. Even before *The Woman In Me* had been released she had had to deflect disparaging comments about her physical features from an eminent source: photographer John Derek (architect of wife Bo's career) had been employed to establish an internationally friendly, sexy image for the former poor girl from Timmins. Apparently he had despaired over her nose. Loudly. But Shania grinned, bared it (albeit with makeup, applied by Bo Derek) and became friends with the Dereks.

Of course the photo shoot offered more ammunition for Nashville critics. She had gone to Hollywood, for Chrissakes, to be pictured! Hollywood! And then by a man famed for creating a 'dream woman' out of Bo. Sniping about the comparisons – John/Bo equalled Mutt/Shania – was rife around Music Row.

The criticism and hostility was becoming almost too much for Shania. Her record label was wholly supportive and label head Luke Lewis has constantly denied allegations of Shania being a puppet in Mutt Lange's hands. Shania in turn has shown her thanks to Mercury Nashville for their loyalty by refusing to be handled by the New York or Los Angeles divisions of her record label. But the vibe around Nashville was too much. She told me, 'Sometimes I feel like an outsider. I'm Canadian, I have a global view of the world, but Nashville is very different. There is some culture shock here and some differences which I understand – but I have been feeling more and more like an outsider.'

Since Mutt has made no public comment on his and his wife's relationship – either professional or private – one can only wonder at what he must have been thinking about the treatment handed down to them by the 'good ol' boy network' in Nashville. For anyone involved in the world of rock music, such a furore over so little must have been dumbfounding. Mutt is a producer. It is his job to make each song, each bar of each song, each note of each bar of each song, sound as good as it possibly can. World-renowned, multi-million-selling recording artists who have worked with Mutt have testified to his meticulousness in shaping their product, yet no-one ever accused AC/DC, Foreigner, Def Leppard or Bryan Adams of being puppets for Mutt Lange. Here was the worst kind of sexism at work. Because she was female, so goes the subtext of the argument, Shania cannot possibly have come up with such great songs or the ideas about how they should sound or how she should look. Which is so ridiculous that it's hard to believe that anyone could hold such a view. But clearly, some did.

Withdrawing from the stark glare of prying Nashville eyes, she and Mutt moved from Tennessee to a big, secluded estate in the Adirondack Mountains in upstate New York to work on her next album. There was some regrouping and a little healing to do emotionally. But Shania determined that all the negativity of the past year would only make her stronger. She knew now that there were millions of people out there who liked what she was doing, and who wanted to hear her. They wanted to see her, too. Soon, they would get the chance.

CHAPTER EIGHT

COME ON OVER

It had taken longer and she had gained more from her last visit than previously, but once again Nashville had forced Shania away. Resident in New York State, she took time to gain some perspective on the career rocket ride that had seen her surpass all expectations in Music City. She and Mutt bought a twenty-square-mile (thirty square km) estate in the Adirondacks, near the evocatively named Cat Mountain in upstate New York. It was complete with its own forest, lake and roads and, of course, state-of-the-art security systems. A few cold miles from the border with her native land, the kid who had dragged through the bush in Canada seeking out food with her father now owned her own forest.

But it was not quite enough for Shania. She was still only on her way, and had not done as much as she might. Maybe, besides breaking with Nashville physically, she had to do it emotionally, too. Mutt was there to take care of her emotional needs (she also had her Alsatian, Tim, to protect her), but she needed to bust out of the parochial Nashville mindset that said country music should be this and that and definitely NOT the other. That mindset would always, she realized, limit her appeal in lands which saw country music as being an anachronism. She could see other female singers, even a fellow Canadian like Celine Dion (with whom her husband was scheduled to work), breaking sales barriers across the world because she was known simply as a singer, not a particular style of singer, just a singer.

How to do it was the question. Her career rise had been meteoric, but she realized that she needed longevity and a plan in order to survive the vicissitudes of not just the country music market but now the pop machine as well. In 1996 Shania made the decision to replace her manager Mary Bailey – the woman who had helped Eilleen make her dreams come true. Bailey was, not surprisingly, hurt and upset and told *Rolling Stone* magazine of her dismay at being dropped by Shania.

It cannot have been easy for Shania to make that decision, but clearly she felt the need to move

Corbis

From Windsor, Ontario to a Windsor at Wimbledon. Shania meets Charles for tennis.

on. She needed professional guidance at a time when a few wrong decisions could make her a mere flash-in-the-pan success and quickly send her into the 'whatever happened to . . .' columns of newspapers and magazines.

Her choice of replacement manager was typical of Shania's refusal to do the obvious. Just as she had allowed a Hollywood actor to direct her second video and had gone to California for a photo shoot with John Derek, she now signed a management deal with an out-and-out rock management team headed by John Landau, who had made his career with none other than rock legend Bruce Springsteen, although he now managed other acts. In a statement to the press Shania – perhaps in an attempt to soften the blow to Mary Bailey – said, 'I'm not the easiest person to manage because I'm independent. If I could manage myself I would, but it's just more than I can handle. I want to focus on the music and the creative end of things, but I'll always want to be involved in every decision that happens in my career.'

It was not just her groundbreaking mix of pop and country, her use of imagery in video and her natural ability for self-promotion that all of a sudden had commentators likening Shania to Madonna. Her sense of self, her ability to detach herself from personal relationships and focus entirely on her career, made her more than a match for pop's material girl.

Shania and Mutt now had to face a serious challenge. *The Woman In Me* was nearing the ten-million-album sales mark, a massive figure in pop music. The follow-up would be expected to at least match that figure. Shania, however, as resolute as ever, was determined to simply make a strong album filled with songs as good as those on the previous offering. It was the right move.

Come On Over was to prove something of a departure from the sound of *The Woman In Me*. The songs were similar in nature, continuing the theme of the sassy woman who is both strong and vulnerable, but this time Mutt was to weave more of his pop sensibilities into every bar of each song. This time there was little obvious pedal steel guitar to be heard and no classic, twanging close country harmonies.

Everyone expected *Come On Over* to see Shania move right away from country music and totally embrace pop music as Dolly Parton had done in the 1970s. And even though Shania always said she truly loves country music, in fact *Come On Over* was far less traditional than anyone could have predicted. She uses French at one point in 'I Won't Leave You Lonely' and utters the very un-Nashville term 'shrink' (as in psychiatrist) in 'I'm Holdin' On To Love (To Save My Life)'. The album's title song features a bizarre musical bridge, which echoes 'In The Summertime', a hit for Mungo Jerry, the British pop band of the early 1970s. Certainly there are plenty of acoustic guitars and two-step rhythms on the album, but there are many more rock-style riffs and big-beat snare drums than on *The Woman In Me*.

Lyrically, Twain continued her US 'Spice Girl' theme. She was sassy, not afraid to speak her mind and addressed thousands of young girls everywhere with her 'wink wink, I know how men are' smile. She was the antithesis of Tammy Wynette's 'Stand By Your Man' persona. But no matter how feminist in tone the lyrics were, the videos countered any threat to the male ego by defining Shania as a country babe, albeit with attitude.

The first three singles from *Come On Over* were hit records. 'Love Gets Me Every Time' and 'Don't Be Stupid' were immediate smashes, but the third single, 'You're Still The One', was key. The song was a lush ballad, only vaguely country in tone, and was immediately a hit all over radio, not just country, but pop and adult contemporary. In the US, where music has to fit into a very rigid radio format, this was groundbreaking. More importantly VH1 and MTV cable networks loved the song and Shania was now more than just a CMT babe. This was absolute acceptance and in a short while she was paid probably the greatest compliment of her career by being chosen for the cover of the rock bible, *Rolling Stone* magazine.

Nashville was now forced to take notice. The barbs and criticisms continued but the movers and shakers were very well aware that Shania was rewriting all the rules. In 1997, Bob Saporiti, Vice-President of Marketing at Warner Bros , was contemplating the future of his label's artist Faith Hill and was keeping a trained eye on Shania. 'She has broken down several barriers,' he told me. 'Her use of video has been outstanding, pushing the envelope just a little, making people think she is controversial when in fact the videos are very tasteful. She has been able to get her music played on different radio formats and has been embraced by a new sector of the market – young girls – the teenage girls who see Shania as a hip older sister I think, who they can use as a role model. She has showed us that breaking the rules can sometimes bring vast rewards. Do not be surprised to see several artists attempting what Shania has done. But at the same time, very few have the intelligence or commitment of that lady. She is one tough cookie, and my hat goes off to her.' Early in 2000, Faith Hill's fifth album entered the *Billboard* top ten straight at number one, knocking Shania off the top slot.

Come On Over sold and sold and sold. Shania had surpassed Garth Brooks as the biggest-selling country music artist. She was having top ten hits around the world, something no other country artist had achieved since Billy Ray Cyrus in 1989, and he was essentially a one-hit wonder – internationally, at any rate. But in Nashville the doubters kept their knives sharpened. In the summer of 1998 rumours abounded that Shania and Mutt had a phoney marriage – that she was using him for his industry nous and he just liked her pretty face. The marriage was a sham, they said, no doubt feeling that their unfounded intimations were supported by the lack of photographs of a marriage ceremony. Mutt's reluctance to be recognized in public – demanding no photos be taken by anyone other than close family – had unwittingly given his wife's detractors another weapon with which to attack her. (For one of these supposedly non-existent photographs, see page 72. Other photos can now be seen at The Mutt Lange Zone website: see Sources, page 96, for details.)

Rumours spread fast in small-town Nashville and the next falsehood to surface was that Shania treated her fans terribly. In my own experience, standing at a CMT Europe function on a boat on the River Thames, Shania gave impeccable and admirable treatment to a crowd of fans. She talked intimately and personally with everyone, displaying genuine interest and warmth and never once looked too important to bother with the likes of what many other established Nashville stars would deem 'just fans'. The nastiest rumour of all, however, appeared in the early summer of 1998 when certain Nashville figures told me they had heard Shania was seriously sick with a terminal illness. There was apparently no end to it. Shania was simply sick and tired of the need to constantly defend her name and reputation, and sick of the jibes about her vocals.

Even living on the same continent as those small-minded good old boys and gals in Tennessee had become insufferable. It was little wonder that Mutt and Shania made the bold decision to sell their New York estate and move to Switzerland. They put up their property for sale for around nine million dollars and headed for the serenity and beauty of a home near Montreux in Switzerland. One of their nearest new neighbours was Phil Collins. The move made perfect sense. Shania, unlike any other country music star, really was an international success and with her husband being a genuine recluse a home in faraway and secluded Switzerland was perfect.

There was still one thing to prove, though. Years earlier she had decided that less can be more in the music business and had avoided touring until she was absolutely ready to do it on her own terms. There had been offers to headline with other country acts like Wynonna and Reba but Shania and her team wanted to hold back. No offence to those two redoubtable performers, but Garth Brooks didn't tour with George Strait or Clint Black, he did it alone. So would Shania. The years of carping criticism of her inability to perform live were based on ignorance. She had been singing to folks since she was eight years old. It wasn't that she couldn't wow an audience, it was simply that if she were going on the road it would be her way or no way. And with *Come On Over* selling as well as the previous album, it was the perfect time to consolidate sales with a worldwide tour.

The tour kicked off in the summer of 1998 and would cover the whole world. It needed to be something special, and it was – costume changes, dancers, an energetic band, lights, dramatics and above all, vocals of the highest order. The dates sold out in minutes. She was the hottest ticket in America and had a sell-out tour within days of it being announced. Nobody who snapped up a ticket would be disappointed.

The show was outstanding. She kept the music moving fast – hit after hit after hit. Shania moved around with grace and energy and utilized the dynamism of her rock-styled band to full effect. Reviewers all over the country loved what they saw. Shania was a star, they all proclaimed, nothing more, nothing less. Her detractors had to eat their words – Shania could really perform. Her vocals were not a studio creation by husband Mutt. Plus she could really dance with the best of 'em and win over an audience with or without all the rock and roll-style anthemic antics which accompanied her. Her years of experience of taking a crowd and winning it over came flooding back and Shania breezed through what must have been a tense opening week.

As the tour continued on its triumphant path in early autumn 1998, the ambition which had prompted her difficult decision to remove Mary Bailey from her position as manager to Shania Twain seemed to have been realized. Shania was invited to participate in a VH1 Divas concert alongside the great Aretha Franklin and the two women whom Shania now counted as her peers, Celine Dion and Mariah Carey. Shania's performance on the same stage as Celine and Mariah was a revelation. Understanding that she could never hope to out-sing those two songbirds, Shania avoided falling into competition and kept her vocals sweet and soft, winning over the VH1 audience with her warmth and naturally infectious charm. That performance, more than any other, once and for all proved her to be a star among stars. She was a bona fide mainstream artist.

As much as the powers that ran Nashville might have wanted to ignore her phenomenal rise to prominence, they could not. Eilleen must have been truly happy when, in September 1999, Shania was invited to perform live at the prestigious annual Country Music Association Awards. The award show, broadcast internationally, is the country music industry's version of the Oscars. Artists dream of winning a Best Male or Female Singer Award, and ultimately the much-coveted Entertainer of the Year Award. As the show approached Shania had sold over twelve million copies of *Come On Over*, and held the number one spot in both Germany and England. Nobody in country music had seen success like this, but while she had been invited to perform at the awards ceremony, the word was that she would probably still be snubbed by the largely conservative country music industry voting panel. Fortunately, the CMA had more sense and viewers around the world, having seen Shania perform in a sexy but tasteful pink cowgirl outfit, watched as she was awarded the newly created International Achievement Award. That seemed to be that until the moment when Reba McEntire, the last woman to win Entertainer of the Year, opened the envelope with the name of the greatest prize winner in country music written inside and announced, 'Shania Twain!' as 1999's Entertainer of the Year. Shania was speechless, breathless and clearly overcome. Speaking afterwards at a press conference she proclaimed her country heritage. 'My roots are Dolly Parton, Merle Haggard, Waylon Jennings and that's never gonna change. But we change, we evolve and we grow and create music of our own – we come into our own. I'm enjoying it. My fans are enjoying it. And I think this honour comes as a nice surprise because I had convinced myself I wasn't going to win.'

Shania Twain was finally recognized and rewarded as being the genuine article. Nashville embraced its most commercially successful artist ever and the doomsayers had to force themselves into accepting that she was in fact simply breaking down barriers, and that would help more traditional-sounding artists to bring their music to a wider audience.

Shania continued her tour, signed a deal with Revlon to promote their beauty products and in November 1999 taped a network TV special for CBS that would push sales of *Come On Over* to the sixteen million mark by the end of the year. She had now outsold Alanis Morrisette's *Jagged Little Pill* and was officially the biggest-selling female act of all time. Internationally the album was charting in the top ten and often number one, even in India – hardly the home of country music. By March 2000 she had sold more than twenty-six million copies of the album around the world. As *Rolling Stone* writer Richard Skanse wrote on 16 March 2000, 'Shania Twain can now lay claim to the best-selling album by a female solo artist in history . . . Presently only four other "single CD" albums stand between *Come On Over* and the best-selling-album-by-anyone-ever crown: Fleetwood Mac's *Rumours*, Led Zeppelin's *Led Zeppelin IV*, Michael Jackson's *Thriller* and grand champions The Eagles' *Hotel California*.'

It was some feat. Twenty years earlier, as a sixteen-year-old singer in small-town Ontario, Eileen Twain had probably listened eagerly to *Rumours*, maybe even performed some tunes from that album and maybe some by The Eagles with Longshot. Now she'd sold almost as many copies as them. The poor little girl from Timmins had fought her way to the top. There had been hardships, tragedies and dramas along the way but Twain had always remained focused on that dream. It might have started out as someone else's dream, but she had come to believe in it and make it real. Her parents' memory remains with her, as she said at the end of a momentous year, after their tragic death: 'I focused on being a singer and kept going until I had enough success that

I never had to worry about where my grocery money was coming from.'

Sharon and Jerry Twain might be astounded and most definitely proud of the phenomenal achievements of the little girl they dragged out of bed every night to sing for her supper in smoke-filled country and western bars back in the early 1970s. But they might not be all that surprised.

As for the future, Shania hinted at one of her career options way back in 1995, when she told me, 'Who knows, maybe some day I'll look to a movie career.' As she took a year out – 2000 – to catch her breath, slow down and think a bit, more than a few messengers from Hollywood producers had found a route to the Swiss mansion she shared with Mutt, bearing potential film projects. At the time of writing Shania had not announced any plans for her future, though. Instead she preferred to concentrate on the simple things in life, allow Eilleen some space to be who she is, rather than be the person everyone else wants: Shania. 'My perfect day,' she told a magazine at the end of 1999, 'would start with breakfast out on the terrace looking at the Alps. I'd wrap a duvet round myself, lounge around, then put on a soup or stew. Then I'd spend time with my horses. I'd come home, have a nice dinner and then Mutt and I would watch a movie.'

Whatever the plot of that movie was, it could never be as interesting, fantastic, heart-wrenching or exhilarating as the story of Eilleen Regina Edwards's life. Nor could it have such a happy ending.

INTERVIEW WITH SHANIA TWAIN JANUARY 1995

Shania Twain's record company, Mercury Records, is among the most modern and high-tech of all the buildings on Nashville's Music Row, the three roads where the music business makes its home. It is low-key, friendly and filled with that special southern charm which makes Nashville different from any other music community in the world. Walking through the Mercury offices, Shania laughed and joked with the employees, catching up on news and trading tales of weddings and parties and Grandma's visits. It is all very unassuming and Shania is perfectly at home.

Sitting in her record company's ornate conference room she exudes beauty. Anyone who has seen her pictures in print or on TV needs to know that in person the images do her no justice whatsoever. She is petite, about 5 ft 4 ins (1m 63cm), I would hazard, and as slim as can be without looking too thin.

In that hour Shania Twain openly and candidly revealed herself to be a straight-talking, no-nonsense performer with an unusually astute grasp of the workings of the always volatile and often unsympathetic music business.

Andrew Vaughan (AV) *The Woman In Me* is very different from your first album. Is this you, is it Shania we are hearing for the first time?

Shania Twain (ST) I certainly hope so. The debut album was kind of a learning experience to me. I was new to Nashville, new to the record business. I was not prepared for the amount of work that went with putting out an album and I certainly didn't have the confidence to fight to have my own songs on the album. There's just one of my own songs on that first record and I felt I had more that could have been there. But I listened to advice and in a way I am glad because I was able to work those songs for the new record and would probably have missed something if I hadn't waited and worked with Mutt Lange.

Corbis

(**AV**) A lot of people were surprised to see Mutt Lange producing a country album.

(**ST**) I know they were. I know I was. Actually what people do not know is that Mutt is a genuine country music fan. He has a great collection of classic country music and listens to it all the time. He was watching CMT when he first saw my video, in London I guess it was. He loves the harmonies and the country melodies. Mutt is basically a song man, and for a long time Nashville has been where all the best tunes are. People imagine that when we collaborate it will be me pushing the country and Mutt adding the rock but in fact it works in the reverse order. He keeps wanting more steel and fiddle and those country harmonies. It's an unusual partnership but it has worked amazingly well and I'm very proud of what we have done together.

(**AV**) Tell me the story of how you two met.

(**ST**) By phone. He saw my video of 'What Made You Say That?' in London and liked how I sounded. He later told me he heard something in my voice that moved him. He tracked my manager down and she told me about this guy who wanted to talk to me. She checked him out with the record company who at least knew who Mutt Lange was, because neither I nor my manager had any idea. So anyway, I started talking to him on the phone and at first had no idea of what he had done in the music business. We'd talk about songs I like and he'd say, 'Oh I wrote that,' or 'I produced that.' It was the strangest thing because he seemed more interested in asking about my songwriting than he did talking about himself. He loved what I was doing and had me sing songs I was writing down the phone. We talked for hours and ended up falling in love. It's very romantic and sounds too fanciful to be true, but that's the way it happened.

(**AV**) Do you feel it's acceptable in country music to be from Canada? Has there been any reluctance from Nashville to embrace you?

(**ST**) I do feel like an outsider. You're English, you can see that Nashville and the South in the USA are very different to what we know. Canadians are more reserved, for instance. And that can lead to people here thinking I am a little stand-offish, when in fact I don't feel I am that way at all. And in country music it has always been difficult for outsiders. Nashville is rightly very protective of the music it has nurtured and developed. But look at Anne Murray, she has had an amazing career in country music. Michelle Wright recently has done very well. I think of myself as an international artist first and foremost. And I feel that being Canadian gives my music a little twist, which makes me somewhat different, which hopefully will be a positive thing as things develop.

(**AV**) Describe the songwriting process for you and Mutt.

(**ST**) That's a good question. I tend to come up with ideas all the time. I write ideas down everywhere I go, little lines here. Titles are really important to me. A title has to say something and be catchy in my opinion. Titles are so important. People just don't know! I write on guitar, come up with the basic chords and song structure. Mutt is great at picking the song apart and immediately spotting what works and what doesn't. He loves good hooks and so do I and he has an amazing ear for the hook. I trust him totally when it comes to melody. sometimes I feel I have a good grasp of lyrics – sometimes I struggle, but I always know what it is I want to say.

(**AV**) People have said Mutt has used you as a puppet in the studio.

(**ST**) I have been accused of all kinds of things. He's a great producer. He's produced hit records for years so people are obviously going to think that. But the truth is that we work together. I respect his experience and he respects my freshness, my honesty and my ideas.

(**AV**) You've become very popular on CMT in Europe. Do you think international is where country music's future lies?

(**ST**) Most definitely. America is pretty insular in many ways and country music is even more insular than that. But Garth Brooks has showed the way by making the effort to travel and play in Europe and so on. There are just so many more people out there to get to. Financially it makes sense to sell records all over the world rather than in certain markets, only in the USA. Being a Canadian I have a different perspective. I am already international as far as they are concerned here in Nashville so I think that gives me a head start.

(**AV**) Who were your musical influences as a kid?

(**ST**) Well, I didn't really know who the people were, they were just the voices I heard on the radio. We were too poor for records so it was always the radio. I got older and found out that it was Johnny Paycheck. That song of his, 'Take This Job And Shove It', was a favourite – it still is. It's what is so great about country music. It has a very direct message and this really cool tune. Then I loved Merle Haggard and Willie Nelson. Tammy Wynette and Dolly Parton were the two women singers who I listened to all the time. But at home as a child we also listened to The Carpenters, and my all time absolute favourite, Stevie Wonder. So there's always been a mixture, but for absolute all time favourites give me Tammy and Dolly any day.

(AV) Talking of Dolly, she was able to cross over, which I am sure you have considered as a possible goal. Are you aware of the dangers that process can involve?

(ST) I hope so. Crossover is what every artist wants, I believe. It's simply that you want everyone to like what you do – it's a basic human element, I believe. In country music you have to be careful not to move too fast. Country music radio is very sensitive to feeling that an artist has used them to gain a platform and then left them for pop. I think some of them turned on Dolly for that reason. But look how amazing her career has been. People know Dolly everywhere.

(AV) She has also been successful with her use of image.

(ST) Indeed she has. Now I'm not going to comment on that in particular, the dumb blonde thing, but it certainly worked. I feel that you need to have an identity. That is all image is. People have talked about my belly button for so long but it's just how I wanted to look and now it has become a trademark. It's nothing outrageous in my opinion. I don't believe I have used my sexuality in a blatant attempt to exploit my looks. I have tried to be sexy but tasteful and classy. If people don't always see it that way then fair enough, but I do feel that I have been criticized for being controversial when I really, genuinely and honestly, do not think I am.

(AV) Shania, where will all this take you, and does success erase the pain you suffered as a young woman when your parents were killed in the car accident?

(ST) Nothing can erase that pain but I learned then how to be strong – real strong. Every day I'm involved in music I think of my mother and how she believed in me. I can't really explain the inner emotions but she has driven me to this point and I owe her everything. She was a wonderful woman.

SOURCES

http://www.shania-twain.com (official site)
http://www.shania-twain.co.uk (unofficial site)
The Mutt Lange Zone at **http://internettrash.com/users/bigbrobasement**
    (includes several photographs of Mutt's and Shania's wedding)
http://www.city.timmins.on.ca
Timmins Daily Press
Rolling Stone
Canada's Hot New Country
Playgirl
Sun
News of the World
Mojo

UK ALBUM DISCOGRAPHY

Shania Twain, Mercury, 1993
The Woman In Me, Mercury, 1995
Come On Over, Mercury, 1998
Wild & Wicked (early recordings, 1989), Neon de luxe/Jomato Records, 1999
The Woman In Me (enhanced version including three bonus tracks and video of
    'God Bless The Child'), Mercury, 2000

BIBLIOGRAPHY

Shania Twain: An Intimate Portrait of a Country Music Diva
    by Michael McCall (St Martin's Griffin, 1999)
On Her Way: The Life and Music of Shania Twain
    by Barbara Hager (Berkeley Boulevard, 1998)